THE BATTLE
FOR STOW

THE BATTLE FOR STOW

ROB WALTERS

AMBERLEY

First published 2010

Amberley Publishing Plc
Cirencester Road, Chalford,
Stroud, Gloucestershire, GL6 8PE

www.amberley-books.com

British Library Cataloguing in Publication Data.
A catalogue record for this book is available from the British Library.

ISBN 978 1 84868 250 4

Typeset in 10pt on 12pt Sabon.
Typesetting and Origination by FONTHILLDESIGN.
Printed in the UK.

CONTENTS

Acknowledgements 7

Chapter 1 The March Begins 9

Chapter 2 Astley and the Aging 19

Chapter 3 Travelling Men 27

Chapter 4 Feeding the Foot 49

Chapter 5 Towns and Villages 61

Chapter 6 Who's in Charge? 69

Chapter 7 Essential Worship 75

Chapter 8 Locals versus Incomers 87

Chapter 9 Jobs for the Boys 99

Chapter 10 Just Visiting 103

Chapter 11 The Last Battle 113

Appendix: The Battle of the Battlefields 121

Bibliography 125

ACKNOWLEDGEMENTS

It would be impossible to write a book such as this without an immense input from the people who live, work, and have businesses in the town of Stow on the Wold; I therefore have a lot of thanks to deliver. First of all a general thank you to everyone that I have talked to whilst writing this book, especially my wife Margaret who has a special role as my intimate local. For information on the Gypsy Fair thank you Alan Lane, Vera Norwood, Kate Johnston, and Mark Buffrey. For help on all aspects of local government (and more) thanks to Robin Jones, John Kennell, and David Penman. For input on the Exclusive Brethren thanks to Terry Mattholie, and the books of Marion Field. For information regarding the new visitor's centre thanks to Sue Hasler. For background information on the closure of the White Hart gates thanks to Nigel Drury and his fact-filled file. For help with photographs I wish to thank David Hanks, John Oxley and the Trustees of St Edwards Hall. And for general information on the battle and the battlefield thanks to Tim Norris and Robert Lamb together with the librarians at Stow Library and the Bodleian Library, Oxford.

For permission to use the cover photograph of soldiers re-enacting a civil war battle, kind thanks to Jayne Carter who took the photo and the Sealed Knot who staged the battle.

CHAPTER 1

THE MARCH BEGINS

Three hundred and sixty three years before this book was written Sir Jacob Astley led an army of 3,000 men out of Bridgnorth, a small town in the county of Shropshire, towards Oxford — then the Royalist capital of England. He did not make it. His journey ended at Stow on the Wold, the highest town in the Cotswolds.

The battle *of* Stow took place in 1646; the battle *for* Stow is taking place as I write — nearly four centuries later. I live on the edge of the town, and the upstairs rooms of my home look out onto a lovely Cotswold scene. In the distance there is a tree-lined ridge marking the beginning of the Cotswold escarpment, which drops steeply into the Severn valley. Closer by there is a much less dramatic valley more typical of Cotswold country and within which I can see the golden village of Longborough — sometimes distinct, sometimes hiding in the mist. Stow looks down onto the village of Longborough, as it does onto all of the surrounding towns and villages. Slightly to the right of my line of sight towards Longborough I can see a steep field recently planted with young trees. This field is quite near to Donnington (a small village which I cannot quite see) lying two kilometres or so from Stow. It is within this field that the battle of Stow took place, a battle that undoubtedly represents a turning point in history since the battle of Stow was the last battle of the English Civil War.

The Civil War has been written about extensively and from many viewpoints. Any attempts to provide a concise overview of the period preceding the war and of the war itself seem doomed to failure, as it was, and remains, a complex stage in the evolving history of England. Imagine a country racked with problems: food prices were soaring as were taxes, the leader of the country was at odds with his own parliament, the Scots were revolting and so were the Irish, religious fundamentalists were vocal, foreign competition was undermining the key industries, and the government was perpetually short of money. Hey, this sounds rather familiar. Today, Gordon Brown would frown in gloomy recognition of these problems and perhaps sympathise with the leader of those days, a fellow Scotsman trying to rule an unruly nation.

Unlike Gordon (I think) Charles the first truly believed that he had been chosen to rule by God, a belief that hardly encouraged compromise. In the words of a Venetian diplomat of the time, 'This king is so constituted by nature that, he never obliges any

View towards Longborough

Powick Bridge near Worcester

one, either by word or deed'. Perhaps, therefore, not the best man to steer the nation through difficult times.

Members of Parliament may not have disputed the king's right to lead, but they were sufficiently emancipated to desire some say in the running of the country, and what is more they controlled the means of raising money — the taxation system. And it was lack of cash that finally ruined Charles' attempts to rule without parliament. Things came to a head at the beginning of 1642 when the king, spurred on by his Catholic wife Henrietta, entered parliament with the intention of arresting the five key men who opposed him. They were not there, 'the birds had flown', and the Speaker of the House refused to reveal their whereabouts. Emboldened by this demonstration of royal weakness, parliament drafted new legislation that would have stripped the King of most of his powers, including control of the army, plus effectively removing the bishops from the Church of England (a particular target for the Puritan dominated parliament). Charles summarily rejected these demands, and so the battle lines were drawn.

Fighting began with a short skirmish around Powick Bridge near Worcester in September 1642, and the first significant battle took place at Edgehill (to the north of Stow) in the October. Neither side were victorious at Edgehill and the King withdrew with his troops towards London there to meet an impassable force, which denied him entry to his own capital. The Royalists then turned towards Oxford, the city that became their capital for four years whilst battles between them and the Parliamentarians raged across the country. During those four years it is estimated that 85,000 were killed in battle and about the same number wounded. In addition to this, 100,000 soldiers and civilians died through disease and pestilence related to the war.

Nothing was simple about this conflict, and one of the mayor sources of confusion must be sorted out right here. The major action of the Civil War did indeed span roughly four years — from 1642-1646 — but there was more. In fact, three civil wars are recorded. The first effectively ended with the Battle of Stow and the subsequent surrender of Oxford to the Parliamentarians. The second took place between 1648 and 1649, it was fomented by the King's secret agreement with the Scots to reform the church — they invaded England in order to restore the monarchy causing Royalist factions all over England and Wales to once again take up arms against the Parliamentarians. This second phase of the war led to the trial and beheading of the King in 1649. The third war also involved the Scots, this time under the leadership of the dead King's son, Charles II. It culminated in a pitched battle at Worcester in 1651 in which the young King and the Scottish army were soundly beaten. And so Worcester saw the last battle of the civil wars (plural) and Stow saw the last battle of the Civil War (singular). Here I will continue to call the first phase of the conflict the Civil War, regarding the second two phases as uprisings against the Parliamentarian government. These phases were bloody and they were hard fought, but history now tells us that all was lost at Stow. Interestingly, the denouement of this troubled time — the restoration of the monarchy — was not the result of armed conflict but the result of diplomacy and the internal disintegration of parliamentary unity.

All wars have an eviscerating effect on the civilian populations involved, but a civil war cuts much deeper. Friends and families were often divided, sometimes by persuasion, sometimes by practical concerns where one brother worked for a landowner, likely to be Royalist, and another for the blacksmith, likely to be Parliamentarian. Many of the

Stow Square from the church tower

common people had no allegiance to either camp, including the soldiers who, having been taken prisoner by one side, could often be persuaded to fight for them. Significant parts of the country were virtually untouched by the war, and some people were said to be completely unaware of the conflict. However, Stow, occupying its critical position on the thoroughfares of Western England, was constantly reminded of the four years of conflict and often acted as unwilling hosts to the protagonists — sometimes the King's men, the Cavaliers, and sometimes the Roundheads.

Stow has been a settlement for many years. Bronze Age potsherd has been found, and the remains of an Iron Age fort can be seen from the air, the fort having shaped the evolution of the existing town. Stow has a well-defined and much admired core normally referred to as the square — though it is by no means square in shape — and has the good fortune to be the antithesis of a ribbon development, the main road sweeping well to the west of the square. The location offered an unlikely site for a town since it is said to have lacked four essential ingredients: earth, fire, water and air! My father-in-law once told me that what grew best in his garden were stones — and I now observe the same thing, more of them seem to float to the surface each year no matter how many you remove. Stow is built on stone and originally possessed a very shallow covering of earth. As a consequence there was little tree cover and hence no fuel for fire. Water has been a special problem throughout the centuries; the main sources being two ancient wells located beneath the town from which the stuff was carried or carted. In truth there is plenty of air — but it does not stay still. 'Stow on the Wold, where the wind blows cold' chant the locals — and it certainly is gustier and chillier than any of the surrounding villages. However, all that said it is one of the prettiest of Cotswold towns; its square is much admired, and the town is visited by many, and quite a few of those visiting develop a desire to live there.

But before you buy that quaint Cotswold stone cottage with its climbing roses and picture postcard garden, be warned! All is not as it may seem. There are rifts beneath the surface, battles that are not apparent to the occasional visitor, tensions that are usually subverted. I am not suggesting that Stow on the Wold is on the verge of its own civil war — not yet at least — or that it especially unique. The undercurrent of conflicts between sections of the community, between residents and visitors, between the town and its neighbours, have their own particular local characteristics — but they also have much in common with any twenty-first century English town or village. It is that commonality that makes this book of interest to all of the eleven million and more people who live in the 1,600 market towns and large villages of the UK. And perhaps it will also be of interest to many of the city folk too as they gaze with desire, disdain or delight at the seemingly idyllic lives of those who reside in the countryside.

Added to these subterranean battles come the critical comments of the surly Scot, A. A. Gill. In his book, *The Angry Island*, he describes the town as the 'worst place in the world'! Blimey! I wasn't around when the book was first published back in 2005 but I'm sure I felt the waves of shocked indignation wafting into Oxford from the Cotswolds as the news of this accusation broke. Dipping into *The Angry Island* I have concluded that the anger that Mr Gill scoured the country for was actually following him the whole time; it is he who is angry, not the English. What precisely caused his red-faced slandering of our little town is unclear — but something got his goat. In his strident and strikingly colourful prose he follows his 'worst place in the world' comment with, 'What

Desirable cottages in Stow

makes Stow so catastrophically ghastly is its steepling piss-yellow vanity. It thinks it's a little smug Hobnob stuck in a tin of dog biscuits'! Ah Mr Gill, some Hobnob, some tin of biscuits. Is there any truth in his vitriolic attack? Are the people of Stow vain? I think that their sin, if any, is pride. They are proud of their town with its enviable square and they know that it's special. Read this little ditty Mr Gill, and be warned:

> They know, you know
> The people of Stow
> Aloft like the crow
> They know, you know

Early in 2009, I left my home in the town of Stow and caught the train from Moreton-in-Marsh to Oxford, my spiritual home, my workplace, and for many years my actual place of residence. Yes, I am a split personality. Though a Gloucestershire lad by birth I have a penchant for the learned city — its life, its buildings, its river — together with a love of the Cotswold countryside — a delightful place in which to walk or simply to gaze. My wife meanwhile is that changeling who in her youth could not wait to leave the small town of

Stow that delivered her, yet in later life returned to the very same town and claims it as the finest place in the world. She is a recycled local and I, as her spouse, have a secondary claim to residency though I will never be a true local. However, I believe my position gives me some qualification to write this book. I would not choose to live in the town, but I am a local by marriage. Through my wife I have links into the heart of the village and regularly witness the affront that she genuinely feels at any criticism of the place and any attempt to change it. She is not a fan of A. A. Gill though she does agree that Stow is a Hobnob in the Cotswold tin of quaint towns and villages.

The rail journey from Moreton is pleasant enough, taking a fairly level and leisurely course down the tilt of the Cotswolds to Oxford whilst passing by villages such as Kingham and Charlbury. Very unusually I had with me a large rucksack with a tent and a sleeping bag attached to it. As I walked from the railway station to the Tourist Information Centre in Broad Street I was pleased to note that the backpack did not seem too heavy. I deposited the thing in the guide's room beneath the information centre and led a walking tour around the colleges and university buildings of the city. That is my job, and, of course, I told my group that Oxford was the Royalist capital of England for four years and of the key event that occurred in my country hometown.

After my tour I changed into clothing more suited to a wanderer and walked back to the station; this time the backpack felt heavier for some reason. I caught the train to Wolverhampton then a local bus to Bridgnorth. And there I alighted in the very town in which Sir Jacob Astley assembled his troops all those years ago, the town from which he began his doomed march to Oxford; I was there to repeat that march.

When Astley arrived at Bridgnorth he found the town 'abandoned and disordered'. This was my first visit to the town, and I found it impressive. It exists on two levels, High Town and Low Town, connected by the steepest inland funicular railway in the country — and that railway is not just for fun, the red cliffs on this (the western) side of the River Severn are very steep. Naturally, I called at the Tourist Information Centre, explained my quest, and asked for any information on Astley, the march to Oxford and so on. The lady behind the counter knew nothing of the march but kindly gave me a file on Bridgnorth and the Civil War, which I examined with great expectations. Sadly it made no mention of Astley, or the army that he assembled there, or his great march towards Oxford — amazing. Yet Bridgnorth was a key Royalist stronghold during the Civil War holding out until the very end when the Parliamentarians finally took over by reducing the castle to an interesting ruin — its keep leans at an angle more alarming than that of the Tower of Pisa.

I cannot find the exact date on which the Royalist army left Bridgnorth, but I do know when the opposition began their march to meet him. The Parliamentarians, having read of Jacob Astley's movements in the newspapers of the time (yes, it's true, it seems that Cavalier security was not tight), set out to intercept him on the 15 March 1646. My walk began on 17 March, and naturally I expected to make faster progress than either of the contesting armies

I followed, as far as I was able, the route taken by Astley and his army. On that first day I did not get far. As darkness fell I arrived at a place called Haddon on the bank of the Severn where I camped in a field beneath a pub called the Unicorn. In that hostelry I had a hearty meal of liver, bacon, mashed potatoes and mushy peas, drank plenty of the local beer, and talked to the locals. I was told that Haddon was now populated

The leaning keep at Bridgnorth

by fishermen, golfers, and visitors to a large caravan park next to the pub. One of the locals was quite entranced with my journey; he told me that he read a little history every night, designed playgroup equipment by day, and lived in a caravan. Everyone was very friendly to me, but I wondered how they might have reacted to a horde of 3,000 soldiers camping for the night.

I retired to my little tent already sensing the early symptoms of a cold, symptoms that were quickly accelerated by a really chilly, mostly sleepless night. I had great confidence in my StormShield sleeping bag with its 'risk range' rated at 'extreme', but this confidence was misplaced. I slipped into it fully clothed and shivered. Perhaps a cold night in March on the banks of the Severn is somewhat beyond 'extreme'. When at last I dropped off I was soon awakened by the dawn chorus and a percussion accompaniment provided by two woodpeckers. The tent was covered with frosty dew. I dismantled it and packed the cold, damp material away as best I could. I felt pretty low.

And so the second day of my walk, the first full day, began. Already I was beginning to get some answers to the question that had launched me on this odd journey: what would it have been like to walk from Bridgnorth to Stow in late March? Answer: very cold and wet.

CHAPTER 2

ASTLEY AND THE AGING

Lord Clarendon, in his famous book on the Civil War, described Astley as 'an honest, brave, plain man, and as fit for office... of major-general of the foot, as Christendom yielded.' This man was a soldier through and through, having spent forty years fighting on the continent — an excellent apprenticeship, no doubt, for his role in Charles I's army. He is famous for two quotations: the second was made at the last battle of the war and I will return to that at the end of this book, and the first was made at the battle of Edgehill, and I find it wry — the sort of thing a 'plain man' might well say. Making his prayers before the conflict in which he served as general of foot in the King's army he begged, 'O Lord, Thou knowest how busy I must be on this day; if I forget Thee, do not Thou forget me.' He was wounded in the battle, but lived to fight many more. Wounded once again in the siege of Gloucester, his god did not forget him even though the opposition had already written him off. Rumours of his death were spread by the Parliamentarians, yet refuted by the following statement: 'Was he slain with a musket or a cannon bullet? Sir Jacob himself desires to know!'

This man was a survivor. Portraits show him as a thin faced gentleman with large eyes, shoulder length hair, a stylish moustache and pointed beard. He could be mistaken for Charles I himself. Perhaps he modelled himself on his king, something that is quite possible. In 1644, Charles made him a baron, and in the following year he became lieutenant general of all the forces in the west.

When Astley fought the battle of Stow he was sixty-six years old! His second-in-command was a much younger man, the thirty-three-year-old Sir Charles Lucas. This man was much more the quintessential Cavalier commander: his father was Sir Thomas Lucas of Colchester and his younger sister became the Duchess of Newcastle. He was educated at Christ College, Cambridge, wounded at the battle of Powick Bridge under the command of Prince Rupert, and recovered to become the lieutenant general of the entire Royalist Cavalry later in the war.

Before beginning my walk from Bridgnorth I contacted the local press to let them know what I was doing. This was not a case of vanity — though it's true that writers often do court the press in the vain hope that free publicity might boost book sales. But no, here I had a specific objective. Given the somewhat controversial nature of this book, I had started a blog aimed at obtaining feedback from Stow residents. I

Sir Jacob Astley (Courtesy the Trustees of St Edward's Hall)

hoped for comments on what I intended to write, on what I actually did write, and possibly suggestions for other topics and battles that I might cover. The results were disappointing. No one commented on my blog at all, so my attempt at an on-line feed for this book was soon in tatters. However, I did get three phone calls as a result of the publicity: one man told me that he owned a pair of Astley's gauntlets, another wanted to set up some kind of study group on the battle, and another invited me to a meeting of the Civic Society.

I include this little digression to describe an idiosyncrasy of the press: whenever they interview someone they always ask the interviewee's age — and almost always include it in the resulting article. I am not sure why they do this but, by this route, my age is common knowledge. At the time of the walk I was sixty-one years old, just a little younger than the aging Lord. However, unlike Astley I did walk the entire distance — he sat on horseback! Funny thing though — clearly I knew that I had provided my age to the journalists, and the information that I had four children, nevertheless I was quite shocked to read these facts in the newspaper. Surely, I thought, a sixty-one-year-old father of four should not be walking from Bridgnorth to Stow all alone in the frosty month of March with only a small tent to sleep in? Perhaps not, but Astley and his men did so in circumstances that surely must have been more gruelling.

I am generally fit and well, I jog a few miles most days or at least take some exercise, but for all of that I felt my age, or rather my infirmity, most in a place called Stourport on the second day of my trek. The cold had finally got to me and I gave up. I had set off from Haddon at about 7.30 in the morning walking through a chilly morning mist to Upper Arley, a pleasant place where the footpath switches from the west to the east bank of the Severn. It has a nice church, a pub and post office cum shop where I bought provisions. Deliberately unprepared for this journey I already had two sources of pain to add to my sore throat and running nose. The walking boot on my right foot was cutting into my ankle and the strap of my backpack was rubbing my shoulder. Still, ever onwards, I hoped to get to Worcester on that first full day and already that hope was dimming — I was progressing at a mere two and half miles per hour. I had taken the path from Haddon that followed the Severn Valley Railway — a popular steam attraction that runs from Bridgnorth all the way down to Kidderminster. This was not a good idea, for one thing it was certainly not there in Astley's day (though it did take the most direct route), and for another it was very up and down and roundabout — not the railway, the footpath. I returned to the flatter route tracing the gentle curves of the Severn Way, it is easy to follow and more likely to have been the route taken by the Royalist army.

My spirits lifted as the sun burned through the mist in the late morning. I began to admire the pussy willow in flower and, though it was cold, I knew that spring was coming. I conversed with the sheep that I passed, but they ignored me. I began to think about the 3,000 soldiers. How long would it take them to go by if you were a villager of Upper Arley and had watched the procession pass through the village back in 1646? I did some mental calculations — I find that they help to pass the time when walking long distances. If the soldiers walked roughly four abreast and, for convenience, we forget the horses and the carts that formed part of the parade, then there would have been 750 files of them passing by. Allowing a reasonable gap of six feet between each file then the length of the army would be about 4,500 feet. There are 5,280 feet to a mile so that's

Bewdley across the river Severn

seven eighths of a mile of soldiers (yes, this is all in feet and miles — no metric in those days). Assuming that they travelled at one and half miles per hour then how long would it take them all to pass by? Don't worry if this sounds like a problem from your school days and you suffered mathematical seizure back then, you don't have to do the sum, I've done it for you. I reckoned that the time taken for the troops to pass by was about forty minutes — quite a sight.

I reached Bewdley at about noon. It is a lovely Severn town and stands in stark contrast to the many small communities along the river's banks that consist mostly of prefab buildings and stationery caravans. I had lunch in a park beside the river whilst drying my tent and enjoying the façades of seventeenth- and eighteenth-century buildings on the further bank. I learned that Prince Arthur had married Katherine of Aragon (widowed, she became Henry VIII's first wife and we all know where that led) in a manor house not far from the town. Rested, but still unwell, I renewed my painful walk along the ever-growing, ever-slowing river.

I arrived at Stourport. This is quite a big place, nowhere near as attractive as Bewdley, but I thought that here at least I would be able to buy a blanket or something to make my future nights in the tent more bearable. I could not. No one sold blankets.

'It's all duvets now dear,' said one sympathetic shop assistant. 'Have you tried the charity shops?'

I did, they seem to sell anything but blankets. I felt despondent and ill. I sat on a wall near to Stourport's very attractive canal boat basin and made a decision. I would cop out. I would take the bus to Worcester. I wouldn't be able to camp in the city so I would find a B&B. I couldn't bear a second night in the tent without a blanket. Surely I could buy one in Worcester for the rest of the journey? I felt such a wimp. But it was very unlikely that I would reach the city on foot, and besides, the soldiers would have been billeted there wouldn't they? Isn't that a bit like B&B? Yes, of course it was. I took the bus. A younger man would not confess to this cop out.

Would Astley be considered old in modern Stow or in modern Britain? Probably not, but in his day he was doing very well to reach his late sixties: average life expectancy at birth was only thirty-five years. Of course many died in childhood: one in three under the age of one and another one-third before maturity. Naturally this was slewed towards the poor and Astley was from an 'established Norfolk family' so would have avoided the abject poverty, overcrowding, and filth that was the lot of common folk of his day. Incidentally, he was not the only elderly soldier fighting on the King's side: the Castle of Pendennis in Cornwall was courageously defended by octogenarian John Arundel. Besieged from both

Stourport Canal Boat Basin

land and sea he resisted all attacks until starvation demanded surrender. His was the last but one garrison to bow to the Parliamentarians.

In the very week that I wrote these words an announcement was made that the last Tommy who had seen action on the western front during the First World War had died. Harry Patch was 111 years old, which, I'm sure, would have astounded Astley. Even more astounding would be the size of the armies. Five million British soldiers fought in Patch's war, more than the entire population of England in Jacob Astley's time.

After his defeat Astley was imprisoned for a while, then gave his word that he would not take up arms again and was released on the surrender of Oxford to the Parliamentarians, subsequently retiring to Maidstone to live with his son. He died in 1652 at the age of seventy-four and, true to his word, did not take part in the fighting of the later Royalist uprisings. Perhaps he had had enough. Nowadays people of seventy-four years and beyond often live a good life, particularly in Stow, one of the retirement capitals of England.

In fact, average life expectancy in the UK now stands at around seventy-nine years, well over double that of the seventeenth century. What a change. And in this year of writing — 2009 — something significant has happened in the distribution of ages in the UK: for the first time ever there are now more people aged sixty-five and over than there are at sixteen and below. In other words the aged are winning, they are inheriting the earth — or at least some bits of it. And Stow is leading the trend here; back in 2001 it already had twenty-six per cent of the population over sixty-five and just seventeen per cent at sixteen years and below. At times this imbalance comes to the fore. Recently, at a funeral, I met a sprightly lady who was well into her eighties. She told me where she lived in the town and that a young woman had recently moved into a nearby house — a stripling of just sixty-two years! Does this imbalance lead to conflict between those who make it into old age and the young who, we are told regularly by the media, will have to support them.

'The very idea', explodes a usually calm retiree. 'Support me? I've paid my taxes and my national insurance stamps. Never taken anything from the state. I've earned my retirement unlike those lazy good-for-nothings who live off the dole. Support me? I've bought my own house, paid mortgages for years. And I've kept the house together; no one from the council came round to mend my dripping taps or broken fuses. Support me? It's me that's been supporting them. Where does the money come from for schools and youth clubs and football fields and universities? Taxes, that's where. I've paid them all my life and I'm still paying 'em. Support me? Poppycock.'

Gloucestershire itself has a slightly greater proportion of retirees than the country as a whole, but the true concentration is in the Cotswolds and particularly around Stow. In fact, thirty-two per cent of the population in and around Stow was over sixty years old at the last census as against a national average of just twenty-one per cent. For those who don't like percentages that's one in three old people in Stow versus one in five in the country as a whole. Why so many wrinklies? Well, why not? It's those mellow stone cottages again with their clinging roses, hollyhocks in the garden, and stunning views across sheep flecked hills. In a detailed survey of Gloucestershire completed some time ago nearly half the households interviewed had a pensioner in residence and, sadly, over 100 of the older people who were interviewed lived alone and had not seen a relative in six months.

Is there really a battle between young and old in Stow? And, if so, is that conflict any different from that in any other town or village? Naturally old people complain that young people are noisy, particularly late at night. One gentleman who lives near to me wrote to a local journal complaining of young women dancing and singing in the street in the early hours of the morning, but I have never witnessed such a display — unfortunately.

There is a battle between the aged themselves. Many are involved in an intense competition to find and retain reliable gardeners. This is a battle that benefits the young, at least those who are reliable gardeners, if any.

There is also, of course, the usual battle between the pubs for clientele and this often splits the hostelries along ageist lines: the Bell catering mostly for the young, the Unicorn for the middle aged and the Queen's Head for the confused. However, Stow's most popular octogenarian frequents all of the pubs and is greeted with loud cheers as he enters some of them. But he is the exception that proves a rule; most of the elderly do not frequent the pubs at all.

It is true that the majority of organised activities, from the local council to the gardening club and civic society, are ruled by older folk and attended by them. This is probably a sign of disinterest and apathy amongst the young rather than a power

New houses for older people — Well Lane

struggle, though I gather that the gardening club can be quite exclusive. Other activities such as fitness training, ballet classes and the youth club are naturally divisive without being exclusive. The elderly tend to get into their cars in order to attend gentle Tai chi classes at nearby Moreton whilst the young get into theirs to travel in the opposite direction to the gym at Bourton.

There are a number of old people's homes within Stow, the most exclusive and expensive being the one almost opposite the entry to my home, Newlands. That there is money in caring for the elderly is clearly demonstrated by the existence and popularity of Newlands, which costs each week for a room in the care home itself more than my car is worth. Oversubscribed, it has recently built an extension of enormous proportions — and of monumental appearance. It is completely in keeping with Cotswold traditions though it does dwarf to some extent the delightfully mellowed and altogether exquisitely proportioned Reynolds Teague almshouses further along the Evesham Road. Newlands also has an estate of attractively designed houses next door. These are exclusively for the over fifty-fives, making the transition between retirement, incapacity and departure very slick.

Though the Newlands development did meet with some opposition, this was muted and quickly subsided. An altogether more controversial development involved a double terrace of houses built in the lane leading to the Roman wells on land that belonged to the local Brethren (of which more later). These houses became known locally known as the 'barrack blocks' since, though finished in Cotswold stone cladding, they are rather featureless and regimented. Oddly enough they are built specifically for the over fifties and yet they are three stories high. Personally I have no problem with stairs, but there is a tendency amongst the elderly to aspire to bungalows rather than multi-storey homes. The specific battle raging around the 'barrack blocks' is not about their reservation for the ageing but their height. The houses are much higher than the original plans, an irony that leads to a true battle — between the planning people who sit in offices many miles away from the town whilst the people of Stow have to live in or with their decisions. This is a battle which I will return to later.

CHAPTER 3

TRAVELLING MEN

Stow on the Wold had no obvious role in the Civil War, yet it became the tilting point in the conflict that raged around it. Its importance owes a great deal to its geographical and road position. Eight roads meet at this small town including two ancient thoroughfares[1]: the Jurassic Way and the Fosse Way (the old Roman road). In the ebb and flow of the Civil War waves of military groups came to the town, some passing through, many staying for long periods.

From whatever direction you approach Stow, on foot, horseback or bicycle, you will arrive exhausted. It lies at the top of a significant hill that has the ability to tire the most hardy of walkers making it an enticing place to rest. The town has hosted weary travellers for most of its life; at one time it boasted more than twenty-seven hostelries, and in 1635 there were fifteen alehouse keepers.

The battle of 1646 brought travellers from a number of destinations. Sir Jacob Astley, as already mentioned, set off from Bridgnorth with the Royalist army, though some records give his starting point as Worcester. The opposition started out from various points, the most distant being Lichfield to the north of Birmingham. Sir William Brereton had just captured Lichfield for the Parliamentarians when he received orders to take one thousand horsemen south to Stratford-on-Avon as part of the plan to intercept Astley. Colonel John Birch set out from Hereford, a city that he had cleverly taken for the Parliamentarians and, in gratitude, had been made its governor. His orders were to march to Gloucester, there to join the Parliamentarian governor of that city, Colonel Thomas Morgan, and then to march the combined troops towards Evesham where it was expected that they would intercept Astley and his men

The troops under Astley, Brereton, Birch, and Morgan travelled by foot or on horseback. Nowadays, travellers to Stow mostly arrive by car or coach, but there are two dates in the annual calendar that do attract hordes of horse-drawn travellers: these are the days of the spring and autumn fairs. Today, the fairs are mostly called the Gypsy Fairs though this is a misnomer and, what's more, a fairly recent

---

1. Many publications also include the Salt Way, but this crosses the Fosse Way well to the south, below Northleach. It is possible that that a minor salt way passed through Stow.

Fairground in Stow Square (courtesy David Hanks)

development. The fairs are popular, but not with many of the locals. Let's delve into a little of their history.

Stow's location at the intersection of all those roads led naturally to its development as a market town. Fish were brought from the River Severn, iron from the Forest of Dean, a wide variety of goods moved north and south on the Fosse Way, and food and livestock were brought for sale from the surrounding Cotswold farms. The Norman invasion provided a fillip to trade in England, and in 1107 Henry I granted a licence for a market to be held every Thursday in Stow to the then Abbott of Evesham (the abbey owned the manor in which the town lay). That market was in operation for a staggering length of time, almost 800 years, and was centred in the square around the market cross, a recognised and regulated place of passing trade. In 1476, the abbot of the day was granted licences for two five-day fairs, one based on the saints' day of Philip and James, the other on that of Edward. This meant that they were to be held around the dates of 12 May and 24 October — the dates still used for the gypsy fairs to this day.

Robin Jones, the mayor of Stow at the time of writing, is not against the gypsy fairs. He, along with many in Stow, wants them to go on — provided they are managed

The Market Cross, Stow

well. But he is adamant that the gypsy fairs of today are not the charter fairs of times gone by. Stow was an important market town and those old fairs provided marketing opportunities of all sorts. It is claimed that 20,000 sheep were sold on one day during the fairs' heyday. Men came to the fairs to seek employment, strange goods were offered for sale from far-flung countries, and the peasants of the surrounding villages came to Stow to sell their wares and to buy whatever they could afford. By the end of the nineteenth century, the fairs had subtly altered, becoming opportunities for entertainment — a fairground being established on the square — and occasions to buy and sell horses rather than sheep. Drawn by their horse-trading instincts, gypsies began to flock to the horse auctions and the fairs became important dates for gypsy gatherings.

Whilst the present mayor is convinced that the fair today is not the charter fair of yesteryear, a previous mayor of Stow disagrees. Vera Norwood is a sprightly lady in her late seventies, sprightly in mind and in manner. She first came to Stow as a war evacuee at the age of nine, later becoming a dancer (a Tiller girl in fact) and later still an art student. She returned to Stow in 1971, buying a house on the square that had belonged to her aunt where she established a shop on the ground floor. The shop sold a variety of things, I remember

Vera Norwood, past mayor of Stow

buying some buttons there when she still ran it and was recently berated by her for this: 'how could I survive on the sale of buttons?' she demanded. Vera is a controversial figure in Stow — and an ardent supporter of the fairs with which she has a long association.

'My very first visit was in 1939. My aunt took me and I can remember her telling me that the motor car would kill the thing off in time', she told me. Apparently this fair was a quiet event, many of the men being called to war at the time — including the gypsies. Her next memory was of the 1971 fair which was much bigger. There were stalls in Sheep Street stretching from the Post Office down to the Unicorn Hotel on the main road; the local council rented the lower part of the cricket field to more stallholders; and the horse auction was held in a field on the other side of the Lower Swell road. The gypsies arrived in droves and stayed for most of the week, parking their caravans on the verges of the Lower Swell road and the approaches to the nearby village of Maugersbury. During the day they trotted their horses around the streets of Stow and at night gathered around their fires gossiping with old friends and relatives.

Vera's recollections evoke an amusing tale related by Harold Bagust. The Maugersbury Road was renovation avenue. Gypsies would buy hacks in the morning, give them 'the treatment', and then resell them in the afternoon. The treatment might involve knocking out a few rotten teeth or even a complete repaint job. One farmer came to the fair on his old chestnut mare, sold her in the morning then went off for a few pints in the King's

The old Horse Fair (courtesy David Hanks)

Arms. Later that day he returned to the fair in fine spirits, spotted a bright-eyed black mare, and bought her for double the amount received for his own horse and believed that he had made a bargain. After a few more pints he hitched her to the cart and drove off home. Along the way he began to snooze, the new horse making an excellent job of finding her own way to his farm. He was awakened near to his home by a downpour — and was amazed to see the mare gradually transformed from black to chestnut before his beer sodden eyes. He unhitched her and watched with growing sobriety and a suffocating feeling of foolishness as the chestnut mare trotted around to its usual stable and started to eat the hay.

Vera told me that everyone went to the fair, young and old, rich and poor. The rich bought ponies for their spoiled brats, the poor bought what they could at the stalls. Everyone enjoyed the fairground rides in the square.

'On occasions there was trouble amongst the gypsies,' she recalled, 'but they sorted it out for themselves with fists or knives — the townsfolk were simply onlookers.'

Then things began to change. The lord of the manor of that time (Kenneth de Courcey living in Longborough) who had inherited the charter for the fairs wanted more money from the local council. He made it plain that if they would not cough up he would bring in commercial operators. Similar demands were apparently made to Taylor and Fletcher, the auctioneers who ran the horse fair. The auctioneers' response was to move the auction to the town of Andoversford near Cheltenham — and so the core event of the fairs was lost to Stow in 1985. Some say it was not the increased charges but the behaviour of the gypsies that caused this move: they were accused of stealing fencing and such. Whatever the cause, the horse fair had gone and this was followed by the demise of the fun fair traditionally held on the square. Opinions vary over the reason for its demise, ranging from a stabbing that took place on the square itself to the increasing acrimony shown by the shopkeepers around the square, there is even a rumour that money changed hands and the fairground people were forcibly ejected! Anyway, they ceased to come — much to the regret of my wife and many other Stow residents who remember those times with affection.

Vera Norwood was a shopkeeper herself, but she did not object to the fair: she loved it. She told me that it was around this time that she met an old friend from art school at one of the May fairs. Dressed a little like a gypsy, a jeweller turned hippy, he announced that he was there 'to fight for the cause'. And the cause apparently was the defence of the gypsy race against the reactionary forces of Stow on the Wold! This particular hippy was an early bird. The following October the fair was full of them, all of them 'ready to fight for the cause'. But the gypsies looked with distaste at the hippies with their dirty habits and amoral attitudes and encouraged them to move on.

One of the things that sets Vera Norwood apart from both critics and supporters of the fair is her membership of the gypsy council (actually there are two councils, Vera's one seems to attract more public figures — including David Essex). I wondered how she had become a member, after all Vera is not a gypsy. Despite this, probably through her outspokenness, she had been invited to take part in an ITV programme on the gypsy situation in the UK. Not surprisingly she spoke up for the gypsies during the broadcast and won the attention of Charles Smith, the chairman of the council and a long-term activist, who was also present. He invited her to join them — so she paid her £10 and became a member. I'm not sure whether or not her membership gives her any influence with the gypsies who come to Stow.

The fair is currently held on a field off the Maugersbury Road, just down from the very extensive vetinary centre (far more opulent than the doctor's surgery — what does this suggest?) and overlooked by the upper stories of the Bell public house. The site, as many opponents regularly point out, is not in the parish of Stow — and thus, they add with satisfaction, the fair cannot be the Stow charter fair. The field is now owned by a group of gypsies headed by a Mr Lovell (Lovell is the surname adopted by a long standing Welsh tribe of gypsies). Vera Norwood's recollection of the acquisition and use of this location is interesting. The old horse auction site was sold and the new owners went to great lengths to stop the gypsies using the Swell Road for their caravans. Attendance dropped, though parking for the gypsy caravans was still a problem. Then a solution was offered by the district council: a field for the gathering located some way from Stow. But the gypsies had to pay to gain entrance and then faced a long walk into town itself.

'Only one family paid to go in', said Vera glumly.

The current field used by the gypsies was then owned by a local man who had applied to build houses on it. The application was turned down so he rented it to the gypsies

The field used for the fairs (November 2009)

for the fairs of 1990, which were very popular with the travellers. In the following year the district council ran the fair in this field, actually laying on water and toilets. Over 400 caravans turned up, some staying for months, and the toilet facilities were ruined. Finally the field was bought by Lovells in 1991 and I think that the battle really began at this point.

Mr Lovell applied for planning permission for caravans to stay overnight on the field, but this was refused, a refusal which was supported at appeal. The fairs carried on and resistance to them grew. In 1996, the district council took out an injunction preventing the use of the field as a caravan site. Though this did reduce the numbers of caravans it was found to be impractical since the travellers removed their number plates and, when approached, gave false names and addresses. And so the battle continued, year after year.

To the travelling men who are drawn to Stow twice each year for the fairs they are a place to meet old mates and family, to sell and buy anything that is marketable, and to deposit litter. To their young women the fairs provide a market of a different kind: a place to display their wares to marriageable young gypsy men. For the older women the fairs are an opportunity to show off their best china and maybe to buy more. For the children the fairs provide an opportunity to express their wildness in yet another environment. For the teenage boys they are an opportunity to terrorise and cheek all and sundry.

To the police the events present costly and time-consuming exercises in crowd control. They sit in their vans at the entrance to the fair site watching the visitors come and go. Occasionally they stop one of the pick-ups and advise the occupants to buckle up their seatbelts — only to watch them unbuckle as they speed away. 'Is this what I joined the force for?' demanded one bored officer as I watched them at work.

To the people of Stow the fairs are divisive. There are those that love them, claiming that they add colour to an otherwise colourless town. Others are ambivalent. Many seem solidly opposed to the entire thing, regarding it as an imposition on their tranquil lives, a threat to law-abiding business and an insult to a sleepy Cotswold town. They would like to see it moved or banned. The merchants of Stow, from the pub owners to the shopkeepers, bolt their doors for the duration of the fairs and count their losses with tight-lipped pessimism.

It will be clear that the gypsy fairs represent one of the biggest of the battles for Stow and hence the subject receives a proportionate coverage in this little book.

Travellers start to move in well before the fair opens, parking their multifarious vehicles and caravans wherever they can since the entrance to the field is firmly barred. I went to see the invasion along the Broadwell Road on the Sunday evening before the spring fair in 2009. It was chaotic. The small corner site bordering the Fosse Way had been settled by a caravan and a motorhome together with numerous cars, four-by-fours and vans. On the opposite side of the road was a traditional gypsy caravan and then a string of modern white caravans, all huddled onto the narrow verge. More travellers were arriving all of the time and a huge van was blocking the road, I think it was a mobile home, but one the size of a bus. It was trying to reverse out of the road onto the Fosse Way whilst other vehicles were trying to get in! Absolute chaos.

Perhaps the chaos helped. I had no idea how to approach the men sitting on collapsible chairs in the corner camp. They looked at me suspiciously as I walked towards them, there were six of them and, though they had established their camp on public land that had been roped off by the police, they had now taken possession. This land was now theirs and they sat comfortably upon as if they had been there for years. I felt like a stranger invading their territory but the traffic confusion left me nowhere to go, besides, their attention was taken by the reversing behemoth. I walked into the camp and said 'What a mess' to a plump chap with a thin strip of beard and sharp eyes. He made some inaudible comment.

'Are you going to the fair?'

'No just passing through, you want to talk to these fellas, they're here every year.'

This seemed odd. Why was he here if not for the fair? I moved along to where an older man was sitting. A tall man, he sat fiddling with a walking stick clearly of his own making. He had decorated the stick with its little T handle by sticking a spiral of yellow insulation tape along the length of it, a simple copy of a barley sugar twist. He was a lively chap with eyes that flitted everywhere but rarely rested on mine. I admired his campervan, a fairly new model with all mod cons. I told him that I had also had a campervan, a smaller one.

'What is it? D'you wanna sell it?' he said predictably with a grin.

'No, no. I like it. It's the right size for me.'

At this he seemed to lose interest and walked away towards a new arrival — someone towing a traditional gypsy caravan. The next two men seemed more jolly, but possibly because the younger of them continually swigged at a bottle of Stella Artois and had another by his side in reserve. I asked if they were going to the fair.

'Bin coming since I was this 'igh', the younger man said, holding his hand a few feet from the ground. He had a florid face, was balding from the front, had a moustache and a dark chin, so dark that it seemed as if hair was pressing through his skin. Like many of the men he talked with a slovenly dialect, much as lowly West Country people do, just as I once did (and still do when relaxed). He said 'bin' instead of been and 'ent' instead of isn't or am not.

I was inclined to say 'since you was a babbie' because my wife swears that the gypsies call their young offspring 'babbies', but held my tongue. Instead I asked him what he came to Stow for.

'See folks, bit o' selling, bit o' buying.'

'What do you buy and sell?'

He and the older, more phlegmatic, man next to him were vague on this. There didn't seem to be anything for sale around.

'Sold all mine, sold the lot', said the older man with satisfaction.

'But the fair isn't until Thursday,' I said puzzled. 'Who did you sell it to?'

He waved his hand generally around the place.

'Other travellers?' I prompted.

'Best way o' doin it.' He said noncommittally. 'Now I can buy plenny of stuff on Thursday.' Was this what it was all about, I wondered?

'When do you move into the fair field?'

'Tomorrow.' And that kicked off an ardent discussion on the time that they would leave, the younger one was all for setting off at 5 o'clock. The other said that he would only have to wait to get in. The main point was that not everyone could get a pitch. Later I heard that there was an awful traffic jam in the town the following morning, stretching right back to the Fosse Way and blocking it in both directions. There was only one policeman at the gate, the others were on their way but were caught up in the jam that they were supposed to prevent! The havoc resulted in fisticuffs between two car owners — they were not travellers.

'Who owns the field?' I asked.

'Dunno. Someone local I think.'

I asked them if they travelled all the time or had permanent homes.

'We're travelling men,' cried the younger man proudly, 'we're always travelling.'

'Where you goin' next?' I asked beginning to regress into my native West Country speech. Dropping my 'are's' and emphasising my 'r's'.

'Epsom races, some of us get together there. Then we'm off to Appleby.'

'Where's that?'

'In Scotland. That's a big 'un. People comes from all over the world to that 'un. 'merica, Ireland, everywhere.'

'What do you think of the shops closing in Stow while you're 'ere?'

'They don't. The butcher's is open, so's the supermarket.'

'What do you think of the pubs closing in Stow?'

'The woman at the Bell says she'll stay open', said the younger man as he cracked open his second bottle of Stella — apparently with his fingers.

'Bloody good job they close,' said the older man, 'save the men getting drunk.'
'Don't you drink?'
'Course he do,' said the younger of the pair, 'More'n most.'
The older man then launched into a common diatribe about the cost of beer in pubs and that he would prefer to have a few friends round, drink cheap beer from the supermarket, cook a bit of meat on the fire by the roadside. He sounded like any disaffected homeowner even though he did not have a permanent home.

We were distracted by the repeated attempts of the van driver trying to park his trailer-mounted, bow-topped traditional caravan (vardo) on what remained of the little triangle of grass. Confused by the narrowness of the road and the attention of his audience, he just couldn't swing the thing around. The older man decided that it would be better to push the caravan back into position. He quickly assembled six willing pairs of hands and in no time it was decoupled and manipulated into position. At the end of all this I found myself next to the first man I had met — the chap with the strip beard. He was complaining that he had green paint on his hands. It seemed that everyone did. The caravan was new and still wet!

The man with the barley sugar stick moved critically around the green wooden caravan, ticking off points of incorrect shape and size, unfinished paint work and so on. He hit the caravan quite viciously to emphasise his point. The owner, a shorter stout man with a thick Irish accent was unmoved. Perhaps the display was all bluster, there was, as ever, the whiff of commerce in the air.

'She'll last me and my boy out,' said the owner, the only phrase that he had uttered so far that I could understand.

Strip beard also took part in the banter and we all moved to the rear of the little van, standing on the edge of the busy Fosse Way watching the son doing something inside the van under the combined direction of three men. It seemed awfully small inside. The roof was covered by green painted canvas, I tapped it and there was something solid below, wood perhaps. I asked the owner what it was.

'It's to stop somebuddy throwing a brick through it', he said, answering the why rather than the what.

I asked strip beard if he was going to Appleby. He thought that he might, he usually did. During this short conversation he admitted that he was a traveller, previously he had been evasive, had implied that he was different from the others.

I walked on down the lane. The right-hand side was lined with caravans, pickups, four-by-fours, dog kennels, and TV aerials tied to saplings. Some of the pick-ups were piled high with stuff — scrap or saleable objects, I couldn't discern which. One had a golden jaguar or some effigy of a big cat aboard, another a gypsy flat cart. Inside the caravans were the women. They looked at me as I passed, then looked away — no greeting. Some of them were dressed in brightly coloured silky material, floosy dresses of another age. There were gaps between the lines of vehicles as if there were communities within this community.

On the other side of the road there was no verge. Beyond the hedge I could just see many more caravans in a large camp on the triangular field that lay there. I am told that a local person lets the gypsies use that field. I wondered who could go in there and who couldn't. Below it were a couple of fields on which horses were tethered for grazing — after all this was supposed to be a horse fair.

Gypsy flat cart in the Broadwell Road

I met a man standing alone beside another very modern motor caravan, similar to the one that I had admired on the triangle. A round-faced fellow of about sixty years with bushy hair and intense blue eyes, he told me that he lived in a house and came here for a short holiday — and to meet people, some old acquaintances, some new. He did not tell me where he lived but he was keen to be called a travelling man rather than a gipsy — though he now seemed to be neither. I think that he had a London accent.

'Gypsies have darker skin', he told me.

He sang the praises of Appleby, and correctly placed it in England, not Scotland. The fair was much bigger, though the village itself was similar in size to Stow. They had plenty of fields in which to park. They were welcomed there: the locals set up barbecues on the roadside and sold them food and the pubs were open and made a fortune. If there was any trouble between the travellers, i.e. fighting, then the police sorted it out. Other people — non-travellers — that I talked to confirmed this view of the northern gatherings. One of them told me that he had once seen a gypsy bring a horse into a pub there.

The closure of the Stow pubs did not bother my London traveller. 'It's rare that I drink more than a pint,' he said. He did not come to Stow for the October fair — too cold and wet. He stated that the fairs had been going on for years and years, implying that they had a right to be there.

'Of course they just had the horses and carts in those days. They used to sleep in benders — a sort of tent made from sticks, bent and stuck into the ground at each end then covered in canvas.'

'Who owns the field?'

'An Irishman bought it. He died, his son now owns it. He's one of us.'

As I came back up the hill I could see gypsy kids in the cornfield, ploughing through the growing corn and flattening it. Tearing it up, and throwing the ears at each other. They were lawless. Many of them smoked. They joined a party of teenagers, youngsters, and babies in pushchairs that were making their way towards Stow, or perhaps the supermarket, in a convoy. They seemed happy enough — I doubted that the farmer would be.

As I walked to my home I thought about the men that I had met. They were certainly friendly enough — but guarded. I was not one of them and I knew it and they knew it. I had felt a little nervous bustling into their world, but that had soon evaporated — besides, what am I saying? Was this 'their world'? They were parked down a road that

Travellers on the approach road to the fair

I regularly walked or jogged along. It was more mine than theirs, but they had taken it over and when I was amongst them I really did feel in a different world.

I had some guiding work to do in Oxford on the Monday, but returned on Tuesday in order to visit the field before the fair started. Passing by I had seen from the road that it was already filling up, though the event did not take place until Thursday. I walked down the steep gradient passing the vets on my right. Just below that I saw a group of youngsters draped over the barred public car park with its intimidating signs, which, in translation, said 'NO GYPSIES'. These were clearly gypsy children; one was sitting bareback on a gypsy cob; she raised her hands and shouted brazenly as I took a photograph of the road with its wobbly line of no-parking bollards. She posed for another photo, cheeky monkey. They were all about thirteen years old — four girls and two boys.

'What you doin' Mister?', she asked.

I didn't have a ready answer so I asked her how she managed to ride without a saddle.

''Tis easy. You just hold on to the mane', she said, but she wasn't holding on, she was sitting on the cob's back with her hand resting on her thighs.

'Are you with the fair?' I asked.

'Course we are, we're travellers', said a pretty girl in a checked coat who loosely held the cob's rope.

'Where are you from?'

'Milton Keynes', said another of the girls.

Then they suddenly dried up — perhaps I was asking too many questions. 'Have to go, can't talk to you now', said the one horseback. But they didn't go anywhere. I wandered on down the lane admiring a similar cob trotting towards me pulling a four-wheeled flat cart driven by a thick-set man dressed in denim jeans and a Barbour-style jacket. His family sat behind him. They seemed quite a load for one horse.

The field is large and hilly, a deep valley cutting it in two uneven sections. There were plenty of caravans, vans, cars and other vehicles in the field and they had already cut roadways through the grass with their tyres. Food stalls were plying their wares, sending up clouds of steam, invading the place with the tempting smell of burgers and sausages. Loud fairground-style music drifted across the valley having no obvious effect on some twenty or more horses that were tethered to the steep sides chomping the grass. Two of them alternated between play fighting and being affectionate. Some of the very smart old-fashioned caravans stood out from the array of vehicles — as if to say, 'This is what it's all about.' The modern vans were mostly sign written with advertisements for legitimate and somehow appropriate businesses such as: landscape gardening, tarmacam drive laying, building contractor (no job too small).

I admired the large sign at the entrance to the field that absolves everyone in responsible positions in the county from all responsibility for the event, then talked to two amiable young policemen sitting in a large white van, one of them was somewhat overweight, the other had discoloured teeth.

'No they're no trouble really,' said the largest one. 'We're just here to make sure there isn't any. They're less trouble than a crowd this big would normally be.'

'People are more scared of them than they ought to be', suggested the other.

I agreed but countered, 'But the shops close.'

Welcoming sign at the entry to the field

'Yeah, but those that stay open make a fortune: the chippy, the Chinese take-away and the Co-op', opined the overweight one with, I thought, some satisfaction.

Another van pulled up. It seems to be full of more policemen — reinforcements? I left them to their riveting work. They were, in their own words, primarily just a presence.

On Wednesday night I did a pub survey — something that I am quite experienced at. It is an eerie sight for a man who conducts pub tours in Oxford to see so many pubs firmly locked and in darkness at nine o'clock on a weekday evening. I passed the Queen's Head, the White Hart, the Talbot, the King's Arms — all firmly closed. The only life on the market square was the Co-op store, still open though a security guard was stationed there dressed in suitable 'I'm keeping an eye on you' attire. I had heard that the Bell was open and hurried down the hill towards it passing other curfewed premises on the way.

The Bell was closed too! What a shocking disappointment. But my journey wasn't entirely in vain. The landlady and her girlfriend were outside the pub with their dogs and, with time on their hands, were happy to talk, though not happy about closing.

'Police told me to. Black mark if I didn't,' said Kate, the crop-haired blonde with piercings who runs the place.

'Got to obey the law. Might lose my licence. I've been closed since Sunday and that costs me a lot of money.'

I made genuinely sympathetic noises as she told me that she would certainly open if she could. She had done so in the past and there had been no problems.

'The gypsies spend a lot more money than the Stow people do — a lot more', she sighed.

A previous landlady of the Bell had told me that she also had opened in the past but the mess that the gypsies made in the toilet had soon changed her mind. I told Kate the story.

'Oh yeah', she agreed, 'got to hose down the toilets after they've been. Pretty shitty. But I love 'em. They sing and laugh and spend. It's the young ones who are the problem, I won't let them in. But there again they're probably no worse than the Stow kids.'

Other Stow people had told me about the vast amounts of money that the gypsies spend when they are allowed into the pubs — but at least one of them mentioned a downside. Generally they ordered in big rounds, paying from the roll of notes that they are renown for — but there were disputes, such as, 'I ordered fifteen pints of Guinness and you only served twelve,' or 'You charged me for three whiskies and I only got two.'

In the mayhem of a crowded bar with customers waving their rolls of notes for service, who is to argue? And there were reports of fake money being tendered.

'Oh yes, I'd open,' continued Kate, despite the downsides. 'I'd take out all the stuff. I've got a flagstone floor – they can piss on it if they'd like. I'd just hose it all down. I wanted to have an outside bar one year. Ordered the beer ready. Then, at the last minute the police told me "no, you can't have, not allowed".'

I asked her if the other pubs would open if the police did not object.

'Well, they're dining pubs aren't they', she replied with a twinkle in her eye. Her way of saying no, I think.

But they have opened in the past — and they are not all dining pubs. Someone told me a story about the Queen's Head from some years ago. It opened and things went very well until the landlord decided that it was closing time. The gypsies did not agree and effectively took over the pub! They peed on the floor (also flagstone so no lasting problems) got behind the bar, in the kitchen, everywhere. The pub did not open the next year. Others tell of memorable nights in the King's Arms with the gypsies standing in a ring singing delightfully. Alan Lane, a drinking friend, told me that everyone did a song, their relatives rooting for them like football supporters as they strain their vocal chords. Alan also told me that a man who seemed to have some power over the gypsies used to arrive about a month before each fair started. He established himself in the Bell and kept order when the gypsies arrived.

As I walked home through Stow's empty square I thought I spotted some lights on in the Stocks, a hotel that has a bar. I don't call there normally because the bar has no real ale — but needs must. The door was locked yet I could see people drinking at the bar beyond the reception area. Thinking that they were residents I almost turned to go when a young lady appeared, looked me over, unlocked the door, ushered me in, and relocked it. I was in. Just one pub fearlessly (well, with a locked door) opened at the time of the fair. As the barman sold me a pint of Stone's fizzy bitter he told me that they always opened, even had a few gypsy drinkers, he flicked his eyes to where a couple of travellers were chatting over their pints in a corner. 'Never any trouble.'

I got talking to an affable, smartly dressed, ex-policeman who had just come from a Mason's meeting and seemed to know most people in the bar.

Gypsy Queens on parade

'The Gypsy Fair has passed its day', he told me, knowledgably. 'The police presence costs a fortune and takes officers away from what they should be doing. And there's the loss to the shops and the pubs.'

I asked him about the gypsies themselves. 'They can be intimidating,' he replied thoughtfully, 'not to me, but to others.'

I thought of my nephew's tale. He had been out exercising the family's three dogs when he came face to face with a group of gypsy youths near Maugersbury village. They stopped him and offered to buy the dogs for some ridiculous price. Naturally he refused. One of the gypsy lads then drew a knife and he ran for his life taking the dogs with him. Was that intimidating? Ask Demis. He also told me that there had been two attempted burglaries at the Stow Lodge Hotel (where he works) during the week of the fair. I asked if gypsies were involved. He didn't know about the first but had helped to see off the second lot at 2 a.m. in the morning. 'They looked and smelled like new age travellers', he told me.

As I walked through the town towards the field on the day of the fair I passed a number of gypsies, including gypsy girls, who were coming towards the square from the field. The girls, ah the girls, they are incredible. My friend Mark Buffery says that the young men look like killers and the girls like chavs. I'm not sure about the young men, but the girls are certainly dressed to kill. Think of very short skirts, long leather boots, skimpy tops, lots of make-up, lots of flesh, and lots of hair. They are on display — but are they looking for teddy boys of the 1960s or for a nightclub that opens at nine o'clock in the morning?

I looked at them with a mixture of awe, horror, desire and amazement. I didn't get to speak to them — probably because of that mixture of awe, horror, desire and amazement, or the sneaky suspicion that they would not want to speak to me — but someone did the job for me. A reporter with the wistful name of Clover Stroud from a *Daily Telegraph* magazine called *Stella* (aimed at the with-it young mum of the noughties, I think) was there and got the lowdown on what she calls the 'Gypsy Queens', which she wrote up in her own pacey style in the magazine. She describes the outfits that the girls wear in a way that bemuses me but yet is so apt, for example: 'Kara O'Reily, in a black net skirt with hot-pink trimming, pink bustler and patent pink and black high heels,' and April Freshwater 'her lids heavy with eyeliner and big diamante hoops glittering at her ears... she's wearing a tiny fluorescent-yellow vest, white pedal-pushers and bright yellow high heels.'

'I like looking flashy. It's my culture', Kara told Clover.

It is tempting to label the girls as decadent whores, and they do remind me very much of the overdressed prostitutes that pose along the roadsides of Spain hoping to be picked up by a horny truck driver. But Clover discovered a very different world, finding that many of the girls were born-again Christians, children of an evangelical uprising that has ripped through the gypsy community over the past twenty years. She interviewed one girl who was unashamedly at the fair to find a husband — but was only interested in gypsy men.

'I never want to marry out,' she told Clover. 'I want a husband to be head of the family, and what he says is law, just like in the Bible'. Later we will see that she could easily be matched to one of the eligible Brethren that live in Stow — though they too marry in. And, like the Brethren women, the gypsy ladies seem to relish their lives as chattels and do not wish to work outside of the family business.

At one point Clover interviewed a young couple and embarrasses the girl, Natalie, by asking if she lives with her boyfriend. The couple explained to her that a gypsy boy would not want to go with a girl who had been to bed with someone else. Besides, gypsy girls 'don't talk about sex', explained boyfriend Matt.

This squeaky-clean morality and clean Christian life does not square with the girls' sexually titivating attire. Nor does it accord with the sightings of fornication amongst the limestone-lined streets of Stow. Are people's imaginations running wild? Not really, I myself have seen a couple shagging in broad daylight within the back entrance to the church, against the lovely door, which is framed by two ancient yews growing close up to the stonework. Were these people gypsies? Evidently not. And there lies the conundrum. If the gypsy community is so clean, so moral, how come such sightings are only made at the time of the fair? Simple, the fair attracts all sorts. The gypsies and their horses are now the core of the event but there are an awful lot of non-gypsies at the event, some good some bad.

I wandered around the field on the big day itself trying to ignore the litter and concentrate on the positives. George Hope, the ex-landlord of the Talbot Inn on the

Gypsy lady with tack

square, said at a public meeting 'Get rid of it, it's just a mammoth car boot sale after all.' He had a point I thought as I stared at a pile of rubbish scattered in front of a traditional wooden caravan or vardo, the van beautifully painted in purple, cream and yellow, the open doors showing an immaculate interior with gold curtains, gleaming china and glowing wooden furniture. The old gypsy lady, undoubtedly the owner, cocked a suspicious eye at me whilst I photographed it. I looked more closely at the rubbish. It was not rubbish at all, just a scattered pile of horse tack — things that I didn't understand, things made of leather and brass for connecting horses to carts. I stepped back and was almost crushed by a horse and two-wheeled trap driven at a furious pace through the crowded field by a maniacal young man wearing a trilby hat. I recalled the warning sign at the entrance to the field. This was a different world to the Stow that I knew.

I passed another vardo even more exquisitely painted and ornately carved. Brass lanterns gleamed on each side, probably copies of lamps from a hansom cab. Above the double entrance door was a 'For Sale' sign and a scruffy piece of cardboard with a mobile number scrawled over it. I could just see a middle aged lady wearing a long white skirt fiddling about inside and went nearer in order to shout, 'How much is the van?'

She came to the door and peered down at me suspiciously, maybe she knew that the question was driven by idle curiosity — I had no intention of buying the thing.

Gypsy cobs and admiring potential purchasers

'My husband will tell you', she responded, then relented and dropping her 'little woman who doesn't know anything' act by saying, 'It's about £25,000.'

I gasped inwardly. That's a lot more than I paid for my motor caravan with its fridge, cooker, shower and what have you. But I had to admit though that her vardo looks much nicer than my motorhome.

I met a lady from Birmingham who was gazing sadly at a young gypsy cob tethered to a modern horsebox.

'Pity he was born', she announced through pursed lips. 'Just moved from place to place. Sold on. See that dog over there? That's a lurcher. He'll probably be sold eight times over during this fair.'

She stooped to pick up some hay, food for the 'pity he was born' cob. She sniffed at it with distaste then pronounced, 'It's mouldy. It's a sin. And the poor creature has no water.'

Unlike me she was something of an expert on horses; she kept show horses and jumping horses. 'Gypsies like the cobs', she explained nodding at 'pity he was born' who had now attracted a group of youngish men. They were examining him in detail, pointing to the hairy feathers around its hoofs, the curve of his back, the patient eyes. He looked like a small carthorse to me. He was black and white and shifting from foot to foot as if embarrassed by the attention he was receiving.

The good old Silver Cross pram

'They like them because they are "doers". I don't like 'em — too small', she continued. 'Those feathers get encrusted in mud.'

Intrigued by her comments I asked the three RSPCA officers who were standing nearby (the only 'official' presence on the field) how the gypsies looked after their horses.

'Oh pretty well', said the lady officer, 'they have to — they value them. They don't like banks so the horses become their bank. Nowadays there's an export market as well.'

I looked puzzled, 'For the coloured ones for breeding', she explained. 'There's a need for heavy blood.' Her attention switched to a young gypsy boy who asked for advice about the pony that he was leading. Something about a halter. I was impressed. They seemed to have a good relationship with the gypsies.

I passed the Silver Cross pram stall with amazement. Our first son was transported in a Silver Cross (a second-hand one I hasten to add, we couldn't possibly have afforded a new one, they were considered the Rolls Royce of prams). I thought that they had stopped making Silver Cross prams years ago — pushed out of the market by the buggy. But no, here they were with their big wheels, elegant springs, and gleaming coachwork. And gypsies bought them. I saw a young mum pushing her baby proudly through the litter-strewn field in its blue and white Silver Cross.

Other stalls displayed the gaudy china so favoured by the gypsies. Colourful and inlaid with gold it was fearfully expensive. Another bank perhaps, if so a fragile one. One of the larger stalls, 'Jim's DVDs', sold recordings of gypsy fairs of previous years! On it a TV monitor showed gypsy cobs pulling gypsy carts across the very field we were in. Why would anyone want to buy these, I wondered? But people obviously did.

Jim, I suppose it was Jim, saw me writing notes beside his stall and had a good moan. 'He's getting too greedy', he cried and I guessed that 'he' was the owner of the field, 'wants £150 a day for a stall like this.' I guessed that you would need to sell a lot of DVDs to cover that. 'And it's not licensed,' he added, 'there's fighting here.'

I passed more of the Gypsy Queens. They not only look like floosies but they chew gum, smoke cigarettes, and posture unashamedly. The Brethren ladies, with who they share the love of Jesus, do none of these things, as I will explain. More than that they keep their heads modestly covered, yet I feel their lives have more in common with the gypsies than have the lives of other women of Stow with either group.

It began to rain — England in May. The pin like high-heels of the girls dug deeper into the soil and the smart covers of the Silver Cross prams were raised. A short man wearing the ever popular trilby hat was selling clever wooden whistles in the middle of the avenue of stalls; they sounded truly bird-like and were priced at a mere two pounds apiece. A group of three youths approached the man. One of them plucked a whistle from his box and began to play it. It was clear he had no intention of buying. The whistle seller tried to grab the thing back and a strange dance began, the youth dodging his every move whilst still playing the whistle, his two companions laughing uproariously at the show. Finally the man muttered, 'Aw, fuck it' and gave up. The three lads, fifteen years old at most, strutted away, one of them still blowing the cheekily stolen whistle. They passed through the hole in the hedge and walked up towards Stow. Intimidating, yes. Law abiding, certainly not. Gypsy boys? Who knows?

I walked home empty handed — there was nothing for me to buy except perhaps a gypsy girl and they most certainly were not for sale. Along the way I met Alan Lane. He lives in the main approach road to Stow from the field. A friendly and tolerant man he does have one complaint — the gypsy kids cannot resist banging on his doorknocker as they pass by! A pragmatist, instead of demanding that the fairs be barred, he puts a sock on his doorknocker at fair times. He's a man with a wealth of stories. One of these described an incident that happened at the very spot where we were conversing. He had been chatting to a policeman during some fair of the past when a gypsy came by at high speed (they do) in his pony and trap. The policeman shouted to the man to stop, he did not, and then, much to Alan's amazement, he saw the policeman leap towards the trap, grab the back of it, and hang on for dear life. He was dragged up the main street, the horse in full gallop and policeman's toes dragging along the road surface. The driver stopped next to a crowd of gypsies who quickly surrounded the trap, prised off the policeman, gently ejected him from the circle and then everyone continued on their way. No trouble!

And so the tales go on. This battle has a long history and it is not simply a battle of the town against the gypsies. The 'gypsies' are themselves a divided group: real gypsies versus traders versus new-age travellers or whatever you choose to call them. The town is also a divided group, divided in a complex way — some for the fair, some against, some of the 'againsts' for it if it could be better managed, and so on. There is an action group called SMAG (Stow and Maugersbury Action Group), which is pretty much against the fair's continuation in its present form and is called SMUG by the incandescent Vera Norwood. SMAG works with something called the Stow Business Association and revealed that 76 of 153 businesses in Stow reported a loss in May due to the fair, the total amounting to over £100,000 pounds. SMAG wants the event strictly limited to one day and criticises the enormous cost of policing the fairs. These facts, together with the tales of threats, sexual licence, theft, mess and intimidation, contribute to a catalogue of resentment that may be large enough to end the fair entirely. Meanwhile, there is a legal argument for its continuation and limitation. If the gypsy fairs are the true inheritors of the charter fairs then there is 800 years of precedent to back their existence and any attempt to ban the fairs may be met with an appeal to the European Court claiming that the gypsies are being unfairly discriminated against.

Perhaps this battle will never be concluded. Maybe the gypsies will simply cease to come because they are unwelcome. Maybe the people who are so very strongly against the fairs will move to other Cotswold villages. Or maybe the problems will continue to be ironed out and peace will prevail in Stow at last — at least on this battlefront. The October 2009 fair passed without incident, but don't let's jump to conclusions.

CHAPTER 4

FEEDING THE FOOT

It was Napoleon Bonaparte who said that an army marches on its stomach — and many will have used similar words before him. For Astley the problem of feeding 3,000 men must have been a major one. To the poor souls who lived along the route of the march, the army must have been as welcome as a swarm of locusts. However, by the year 1646 they were probably used to it. Troops of both sides, some small in number, some large, had moved around the country for the previous four years demanding food and shelter. There cannot be a much better example of the privations imposed on the better-off than the experience of John Chamberlayne, Lord of the Manors of Stow and Maugersbury at the time.

Chamberlayne was a significant landowner and a Royalist with a brother who served as a colonel in the king's army. Regardless of his sympathies he was expected to provide hospitality for both sides of the conflict and pay regular amounts to fund the opposing armies. And when his side lost the victorious Parliamentarians attempted to sequester his entire estate. In pursuing his defence he provided detailed summaries of what the war had cost him — a total of £446 10s 4d (maybe £¾ million in today's money). Here are some of the things the poor (!) man had splurged out on during the war. He had forty different groups of visitors, some welcome, some not, all in search of a bed and food but with no money to pay for them. At the end of the war he reckoned that he had fed, watered and boarded 63 officers, 742 men, and 309 horses. On one occasion alone he accommodated 150 officers and men plus their 40 horses. These were from Sir William Waller's army and they stayed for five nights. Others stayed for longer. One group of five soldiers stayed for fifty-one nights with their horses — what were they up to I wonder?

Landowners like Chamberlayne had little choice in all of this. If a group of well-armed soldiers turned up at your door asking for bed and board for the night you might be inclined to call the police or at least complain to your MP. But 'When Civil War begins, the "King's Peace" is at an end, the Law is forgotten or despised, the whole body politic is in a state of fever, and the usual functions of orderly government are suspended.' Chamberlayne had to put up, shut up, or pay a considerable amount in bribes to persuade unwelcome callers to try elsewhere. Naturally he made a note of all of these bribes and included them in the bill when attempting to protect his estates.

There were other items in that bill. Forage parties arrived demanding provisions for their respective armies, and if provisions were not given they were taken. He lost crops from the fields, sheep from their folds, and bread, beer, cheese, and meat was stolen directly from his own stores. Added to all of this was the damage caused to his estates by the opposing forces. 'I had corn upon the ground spoiled by the two armies — Prince Rupert facing my Lord the Earl of Essex at Stow — worth £40 at the least', and 'When Sir Wm Waller lay at Stow, the carriage horses were turned in my corn and did me at the least £30 worth of hurt.'

Undoubtedly Chamberlayne did suffer a lot of hurt, but poorer people often fared worse — for them a visit by a raiding party could mean ruin. A farmer's only horse might be taken, together with his store of seed corn. The result is clear — next season he would have no horse to put to the plough and no seed to put to the field. Ordinary people suffered too. Thomas Tasker of Epwell, a village then in Oxfordshire but near the border with Warwickshire, was a labourer and an 'aged' one at that. His home was raided in the middle of the night by the soldiers of Major George Purefoy, a commander in the Parliamentarian army based in Warwickshire and, according to the records of the Committee of Accounts, they took:

> ... in money 10s, 7 pairs of sheets, 3 brass kettles, 2 brass pots, 5 pewter dishes and other smaller pewters, 4 shirts, 4 smocks, other small linens, 2 coats, 1 cloak, 1 waistcoat, 7 dozen of candles, 1 frying pan, 1 spit, 2 pairs of pot hooks, 1 peck of wheat, 4 bags, some oatmeal... and whatsoever else they could lay their hands on.

The court was petitioned for the return of the goods since 'he and his wife are aged, and the sudden fright hath made them both so sickly and weak that they are altogether unable to get their living'. I can't help thinking that this seems quite a lot of stuff for a seventeenth-century labourer to own, but I suppose a degree of inflation in these claims was inevitable from any but the most honest of petitioners.

A foot soldier called Henry Foster (coincidentally this was my father-in-law's name) who was marching with the Royalist army from London through Gloucestershire recalled standing in the open fields all night near Stow. They were expecting an enemy attack and 'having neither bread nor water to refresh ourselves, having also marched the day before without sustenance, neither durst we kindle any fire, though it was a very cold night.' And there was little sustenance as they marched on through villages already packed full with soldiers. Some ran ahead of the main army to feast on what little they could find before the hordes arrived. By the time the march came to a halt in a field near Prestbury some complained that 'they had not ate or drunk for two days'.

Royalist leaders were supposed to provide their troops with two pounds of bread, one of meat and two pints of beer each day to give the men sufficient energy to fight. This was rarely available so troops were often billeted in local houses and they then expected the householders to feed them. The soldiers had to pay for their food from their own wages or provide what was in effect an IOU signed by them. Where things were well organised, farmers and shopkeepers established markets that followed the troops on their meanderings through the countryside.

'There would be little for them to eat at this time of year', I mused in my notebook after consuming a sausage roll and a few biscuits purchased from the shop cum post office at Upper Arley. There were fish in the river of course, and ducks and geese, there were also rabbits and, of course, sheep in the fields, but you would need to catch, shoot or trap an awful lot of them to feed the 3,000. Just before Bewdley I met a woman exercising four dogs.

'Are all of these yours?' I asked whilst petting the friendliest pair.

'I've got two more at home,' she said, sniffing into a tissue (she too had a cold).

'It must cost you a fortune to feed them all.'

'Not really, about £20 each week', she sneezed, and then passed on in the direction from which I had come.

Did the soldiers eat dogs? Six of them would have provided a decent meal but would be lost amongst the 3,000. In fact a whole cow would be lost amongst such a crowd. One cow yields roughly five hundred and fifty pounds of edible meat, so to give the soldiers their ration of one pound of meat per day it would have been necessary to slaughter six of the beasts. If their fancy turned to pork then eighteen pigs must meet their end, or mutton then a herd of some ninety sheep would need to be killed and prepared.

There were plenty of trees around as I walked, but no nuts, no fruit, and nothing on the bushes either. Later I was to pass through agricultural land, especially in the Evesham area, but even here there was little in the fields — turnips and leeks were the only things that I saw that could be eaten. Astley must have relied heavily upon the food they had brought with them in carts and on the likes of Chamberlayne to feed his 3,000. The numbers are staggering, and remember that Astley led only a small army.

I had to buy my food as I travelled and there were always supermarkets along the way, often those little ones that are so much less daunting than the large Tesco store at Stow. Breakfast consisted of a cereal bar, a banana and a biscuit or two, washed down with a carton of fruit juice — though on my cheat stay in the B&B in Worcester I indulged in a full English breakfast, and golly that was good. For lunch I might have a Cornish pasty and a pear, swilled down with water. In the evening I dined in any convenient pub that served real ale. I probably spent about £10 per day on food — excluding ale of course (an unnecessary indulgence perhaps, but remember that the soldier's recommended ration was two pints per day). Apart from a hot toddy for medical purposes I cannot remember taking a hot drink at all during the journey and I did not miss it. I enjoyed my food enormously. Lunch was the high point of the day and dinner that of the evening.

I needed food, really needed it. The combination of entire days in the open air and the relentless plodding along with all my worldly goods strapped to my back made me quite ravenous. I ate well and drank well. The only thing that I envied the soldiers of nearly four hundred years ago was fire. Undoubtedly they collected wood as they travelled and lit bonfires at night — at least when the enemy was not at their heels. The fires were essential to cook their food, and the warmth would have been so welcome — they did not even have a StormShield sleeping bag with its 'risk range' rated at 'extreme'. I suppose that I too could have lit campfires — but in two of my three campsites building an open fire would have been an act of vandalism. I attempted to leave everything exactly as it had been, apart from a flattened patch of grass. I took nothing and I left nothing, and no one could tell that I had passed through.

In modern day Stow there is no shortage of food. The battles rage between the competing food outlets, eating in or eating out, buying organic or chemical and the desire of many residents to maintain the traditional variety of shops and markets against the dominance of the modern supermarket.

Setting up the farmers' market

Stow-on-the Wold no longer holds a weekly market, but there is a monthly farmers' market. This is a phenomena that has hit many places in the UK — it provides a means of getting wholesome farm-fresh food direct to the shopper without all of the packing, central distribution and so on which characterises the modern day food chain. I talked to one of the stallholders, a lady who farmed in nearby Evesham. She told me that business was good, especially when a 'granny bus' arrived in the square. She told me that many of the tourists loved to browse the stalls and that they do buy farm goods to take home. I asked her if the nearby supermarket took away her trade. 'Oh no,' she said smiling, 'people like something different, different from all that pre-packed stuff.' I wondered what she had that was different and she showed me some Swiss chard leaves and told me how to cook it. I bought some — but didn't like it much. The stalls are colourful; they are laid out in front of the famous stocks so that you can buy tomatoes and such to throw at the miscreants with their feet locked into the heavy boards. But there are no miscreants to pelt nowadays, or if there are then they are no longer placed in the timeworn stocks. The stalls of the farmer's market certainly brighten up the square and are the only regular glimpse of the Stow's heyday as a market town.

Tesco supermarket, Stow

Stow's large supermarket broodily overlooks its own convenient car parking on the main road, the Fosse Way, barely five minutes walk away from the square. Though there may be no real battle between the farmers' market and Tesco, there was a furious battle over the establishment of a supermarket on this spot. This is a battle that has echoes through many of the towns and villages of England. Supermarkets, especially the larger ones, can and do kill trade in the traditional centre of communities — though, in fairness to the operators of these places, all they really do is offer a choice. It is the shoppers themselves who desert the delights of the older style shops to enjoy the convenience of an emporium that sells almost everything in the grocery line (and more) under one roof. It is the shoppers who enjoy buying at the cut prices that economies of scale produce — prices that the little shops cannot match.

The battle with Tesco took place in the late 1990s, and planning permission was finally granted for a store in 1997. This battle has some resonance with the Civil War since it split the community of Stow: some people were staunchly against the development, while others were decidedly in favour. And the scars remain, there are still those that will not set foot in the place and yet others who are disappointed by it. The battle may have lacked blood and gore but it was certainly vicious and spirited.

The planning application was turned down seven times! At the final meeting the local planning officer urged councillors to approve the proposal or face the heavy costs of an appeal — warning that each of them could be personally liable for those costs.

Thus bullied into submission, the councillors passed the plans. But that was not the end of the battle. There was a public enquiry and a group of local people used their own funds to take the decision to judicial review, and when that failed they appealed to the House of Lords. What worried them about this development so much? They feared for the local stores on Stow Square, the butcher's, the cake shop, the greengrocer's and so on. They feared for the entire future of Stow as a commercial centre. Were their fears grounded? Let's have a look at some follow up reports and comments.

In 1999, the *Daily Telegraph* published an article prophesying that Stow would become some sort of theme park, a sort of 'villageworld' with actors playing the parts of blacksmiths and sheep shearers. I don't think that it has happened, though I do have some doubts about the postman, he is so efficient, so friendly. For me the real meat of the *Daily Telegraph* article is when it began to focus on reality and to survey the aftermath of the opening of Tesco, noting that after just eighteen months a butcher's and a greengrocer's had closed. Here are some other relevant comments from that time:

Judy Shaw of Smalley's, the hardware store, had something to say about the change in shopping habits. 'We've been here for twenty years and there have certainly been fewer people in the shop recently. It's hard to tell whether that is because of Tesco or the general dip in shoppers. One thing we have been forced to do is diversify. We now do film developing and we've started selling lots of seeds for the American tourists who like to take flowers home.' Sadly Judy closed her shop a few years later.

Helen Finlay, manageress of Maby's, the Stow deli, was more forthright. 'We have had a really bad year and can only assume that Tesco is the reason', she said. 'We really don't see as many people down here as we once did. Everyone is complaining that business is not good and we are no different.' Maby does still sell food in Digbeth Street.

Michael Sharpe was the secretary of Stow's Chamber of Commerce and had a shop in the centre of the town. He resigned from the Chamber as a protest against the supermarket group being allowed to join and had plenty to say about the long term effect of the development: 'Tesco will alter the style of the village and this is one of the points I made at the public inquiry. The square will no longer be a meeting place for the community and that is already being seen. Food shops have already closed.'

'Several planning applications for the area had been turned down before. The problem now is how do you stop anything else going up? Tesco sets a precedent. The next thing we will see is applications for developments next to Tesco. The farmers will be sitting there looking at what is going on with great interest. Eventually there will be ribbon development and then the village will have gone completely.' So far Michael's dire prophecies have not transpired — but see the later chapter on the Brethren where a threat to the adjoining land is described.

George Hope, the sadly missed landlord of The Talbot on the market square, characteristically had a different angle on the Tesco effect:

Small communities are always under threat, but the biggest threat to the life and times of Stow on the Wold is not Tesco, it's gift shops pandering to the coach traffic. Gift shops take over shops that could be proper shops serving our community because

The Talbot at Christmas

property owners go for high rents, which only gift shops can afford. We used to have a proper little sweet shop here with jars of humbugs and chocolate-coated raisins and that's now a gift shop. There is not a governing body to stop the advancement of gift shops. Even in tiny places the rent is getting on for £20,000 a year.

George still visits Stow so he will be pleased to note that a sweet shop pretty closely fitting his description has been re-established on the square.

The *Daily Telegraph* article is fair, it gave the microphone to Tesco spokesperson Nicole Lander: 'We spent four months researching the site,' she said, 'and from this it was evident that people were driving many miles to other stores, so we identified a trading opportunity. There was a support group in the town made up of people who felt that Stow offered nothing unless you were rich or American and some locals campaigned for the store.'

Asked about the effect of the supermarket on the local shops she said:

I would be immensely surprised if we had any effect on the shops in Stow. We are actually in competition with our other stores. If anything, we stop people driving away from Stow. We want the shops of Stow to trade alongside us. We all have a responsibility, we're not mindless automatons.

In 2005, *The Times* published an article based on a proposed new Tesco store at Gerards Cross. Local people were opposing the development and the journalist chose Stow as a precedent for the new development. The article began by reporting the undeniable success of the store.

'It's great', said Shirley Hall, who lives in the nearby village of Oddington where the only shop closed several years ago. 'Shopping was bloody awful in Stow before Tesco came.'

But not everyone was so upbeat, Aloyse Packe's views had changed over time:

When Tesco came I was quite pleased — I thought it would make my life more convenient and you could buy sundried tomato paste, which everyone seemed to need at that time. But now I find it terribly boring: the fruit and vegetables are disappointing and I have to go further afield again.

The Times article commented on the closure of local shops following the opening of the supermarket and gave space to others traders who were hurt in a different way. Janet Smith, a local dairy farmer, claimed that Tesco did not pay a decent price for anything, especially milk. 'They have such a stranglehold that they are taking the livelihoods from farmers. But I shop there like everyone else — mainly because of the parking.'

Following this theme, the article had a good poke at the diversity of Tesco's supply chain with its resultant shunning of truly local sourcing.

It is ironic that in an urban conglomerate such as London, miles from the nearest orchard or greenhouse, we can get practically anything we want: Gloucester Old Spot pork, hand-picked purslane, Kent greengages: a vast choice of fresh, fully traceable English produce. Meanwhile, in a market town like Stow, which once echoed to the bleating of sheep and the cry of the auctioneer and is surrounded by richly productive Cotswold pasture and arable land, there is a hardly a locally grown broad bean or strawberry in sight.

Eating out is as popular in Stow as it is in any other town in England — more so perhaps because of its location and consequent draw for tourists. I estimate there are over 500 dining seats in cafés, restaurants, pubs and hotels in the town. That seems quite a lot: the whole town could be fed in four sittings and Astley's army in six. The battle here is the usual competition between hostelries. Some beckon the rich in terms of price and quality, some target the tourists, particularly the cafés and pubs, and others are simply middle-of-the-road eateries or pubs. And, of course, for those who do not aspire to a night out there is a very good chippy and, its competitor of sorts, a Chinese take-away.

There exists a group of shifty people in Stow, and I'm one of them. We move from pub to pub looking for... I don't know what: better beer, better company, or perhaps just for the joy of pub-crawling? I have already mentioned the most famous of the shifters. His name is Cyril and he is my hero and role model for the future. He is a tall man approaching his eightieth year and tours the pubs of Stow on most nights. He is so popular that a cheer goes up throughout the bars of some of the pubs when his tall frame passes through the entrance. He once operated a garage on the main street and tells me that his father owned many houses in the town that he rented out. Many years ago most of them suffered in the battle to clean up Stow, they were condemned as unfit for human habitation and effectively confiscated. That aside Cyril could now be an important member of the landowner class in the town. He has born in a small house that existed in the alleyway beside the King's Arms and maybe his upbringing influences his nocturnal wandering to this day; long may those wanderings continue.

There is one drinking establishment that does not belong to the usual pub/hotel category in Stow. A friend calls it the 'reservation' and it is almost entirely the bailiwick of locals, true born and adopted. This place is the British Legion club, an extensive modern building with a skittle alley, two pool tables, darts and so on. It is one of the main centres of entertainment — live bands often sweeping the members to their feet. John Entwhistle played in the Legion on one memorable occasion. John was the bass player of the Who and, in company with many famous entertainers, used his lucre to purchase a massive stately home in the Cotswolds. He lived quite near to Stow and was persuaded to play his legendary elongated bass guitar with an aging local group called, imaginatively, the Stowaways. John was quite deaf by this point in his life and the sound generated by his bass shook the bar of the British Legion Club so much that it buzzed. Nobody dared complain though.

John Entwhistle's fame has survived his cocaine-induced death at the Hard Rock Hotel in Las Vegas in 2002. His funeral service was held in the church at Stow and the

The Queen's Head

landlady of the Bell Inn named her front bar in his honour. This is the bar where the youngsters of the town congregate to play pool, the only pool-room in town besides the Legion.

The British Legion has other roles within the community apart from providing an alternative drinking hole, particularly the charitable support of old or maimed soldiers and their families. The clubroom is also used as a popular location for wakes. I have attended at least three of these affairs over the years; they followed the funerals in St Edward's church and the burials in the overflowing cemetery alongside the Fosse Way. The wake is usually accompanied by a grand finger buffet, beer and reminiscences. For the deceased it is an appropriate place to end since many of them would have spent a good deal of their lives there.

The Legion is the focus for a battle of sorts. Here the contenders choose between a club that offers cheap booze and entertainment for a membership fee and the pubs that provide an entirely different ambience but maintain higher prices. Once again this is a battle that is encountered throughout England. It is a battle that is waged within a greater war: the war of the missing drinkers. Social habits have changed and pubs and clubs are no longer central to most people's lives. Locally the main enemy is Tesco. It is far cheaper to buy beer or wine in the supermarket and drink at home in front of the TV screen rather than venture out to the pub or club. At home you can choose your own entertainment, smoke if you wish to, close when you want to, refuse entrance to people that you dislike and generally have fun!

CHAPTER 5

TOWNS AND VILLAGES

Though Astley and I would have passed through many of the same towns and villages, I was aware of some very major changes. Stourport (the town in which I copped out and caught the bus to Worcester), for example, just wasn't there in his day. It is a creation of the canal era coming to life in 1772 then growing rapidly through its importance as an inland port. And of course those little caravan villages that I passed alongside the Severn were so recent that they hardly had names — and may well be a temporary phenomena. Worcester was the easily the largest place that I passed through. As already mentioned it was a significant city in Astley's day, and a Royalist one at that. It has many fine buildings still surviving from the seventeenth century, including the handsome Guild Hall with its carving of Cromwell above the front door. He is portrayed as the devil with his ears pinned to the wall, and below him and on each side of the doorway are the imposing statues of two kings — Charles I and II. Yes, this was certainly a Royalist stronghold.

Upon leaving Worcester I was faced with a dilemma. The next recorded location for Astley and his army was Evesham, but he did not cross the river Avon there. Instead the town presented him with two disappointments. On the far banks of the river he saw the army assembled by Morgan and Birch. He had no wish whatsoever to engage them: his job was to get to Oxford with his rescuing army intact. What is more, the bridge over the river had been destroyed in the previous year — by his own people. The two sides of the conflict were now within sight of each other and were faced with a strange impasse. Morgan's orders were to stop Astley; Astley's orders were to relieve his king. In the event, Jacob Astley decided to stay on his side of the river rather than battle it out with the Morgan, even though the Parliamentary combined strength was smaller than his own. He marched up and down the river, presumably searching for a way through to Oxford without a clash of arms. The impasse ended when Morgan withdrew towards Chipping Campden where he could watch the Royalists' progress from the heights of the Cotswold escarpment. He hoped that his withdrawal from the river would encourage Astley to cross over and he was rewarded — on 19 March 1646, the Royalist army finally made the crossing at Bidford-on-Avon.

My decision, as I stood on the edge of the city of Worcester near to the County Hall, was where should I go? I felt much better; my cold had benefited enormously from a

Cromwell as the devil, Worcester Guild Hall

night in a warm B&B and I had bathed my feet a couple of times in hot salty water using the small basin in my room. A hot shower had also helped. Heat is the only way to counteract colds. I perused some old maps of the seventeenth century, and the most direct route to Evesham seemed to coincide with the main road, which passed through Pershore. This was not an attractive route for me. The troops of long ago would have found the road quiet, they might have met the occasional trader, or farmers going to market, or workers on their way to distant fields. But for me the route presented many hours of walking alongside a busy main road accompanied by the roar of lorries and the angry swish of motor car tyres speeding over the metalled road. What's more, that route would bring me out on the wrong side of the river. I could be captured by Morgan and his men and held as a Royalist spy! I had just crossed the M5 motorway and looked down from the bridge across it with profound distaste. This was a far cry from the pleasant walk I had taken alongside the Severn. I decided to make straight for Bidford, after all this was the next important staging post in the Royalists progress. I intercepted an old road that led to Piddle having first followed the Stratford road away from Worcester.

One thing that I observed on this trip, something that I have noted on other walking or cycling tours, is just how quiet our villages are. As you pass through them it is quite

Busy Stow

easy to believe that these places are actually deserted. This would not have been so at the time of the Civil War. The prime, if not the only, occupation was agriculture and its support so the fields and villages would have been very active places. In late March the activity would have focused on raising the winter vegetables and preparing the soil for spring and summer plantings. The date of 21 March, or thereabouts, is generally recognised as the day to plant early potatoes, in those days a new crop from South American. Village greens would have been used to pasture animals and there would have been a plethora of time-consuming maintenance tasks to do involving the land, the hedges, the walls, and the buildings. Nowadays many of the tasks that would take a week or more are completed in less than a day by one man and a tractor, and many of the villages are pleasant dormitories for people who work in the towns, cities and industrial estates.

Stow on the Wold, on the contrary, is rarely deserted. As the 'capital' of the Cotswolds and the highest inhabited point it is a busy little place. However, its altitude is no guarantee of supremacy — the place is surrounded by competing towns and villages all of which battle it out for tourists, shoppers, jobs, hospitals, and fitness facilities. In the proximity of Stow there are a number of small villages which look to it as a centre, the obvious ones being Maugersbury, Broadwell, Longborough, Donnington, the Swells

(Upper and Lower), and the Oddingtons (Upper and Lower). These are villages mostly without shops and sometimes without the benefit of a pub. The residents have to come to Stow for their groceries, postage stamps, hardware, clothing, and so on. There is no battle here, more of a synergy. However, once the proud owner of a limestone cottage in, say, Lower Swell is seated in his Range Rover contemplating a shopping trip, he or she can as easily drive to one of the other market towns in the area rather than Stow. Moreton (in Marsh) and Bourton (on the Water) are the main competitors. Moreton boasts a railway station, an irresistible plus for some. Of course, Stow had one once, as did Bourton. Bourton's station was pretty near to the centre of the town, but Stow's was not. In fact, Stow's station was so far from the town that children on a day's outing to Cheltenham thought that they were walking the whole way. This was one disadvantage of being the highest town in the Cotswolds, as the old steam train couldn't get up there. The abhorrent Beeching cuts of the 1960s saw the demise of the Great Western Railway's Banbury and Cheltenham Direct Railway line, one of the most beautiful in country — the route is still evident in places. Trains ran from Kingham to Cheltenham about six times a day. The journey from Stow to Cheltenham took about three quarters of an hour.

Besides its enviable railway link, Moreton also retains a weekly market, has an agricultural show once each year and boasts a supermarket, a hospital, and a town hall of sorts. What it lacks is tourists. It has plenty of handsome limestone buildings and a good selection of pubs and restaurants together with an award winning teashop. But it's flat, it does not have the views, and what is the Cotswolds without views? Talking to Sue Hasler, who appears again later in this book, I discovered that she lives in Moreton but has a bookshop in Stow. I asked her why.

'Moreton offers the best value for money in terms of housing,' she said. 'It's a nice place to live, but Stow, with its lovely square and droves of tourists, is the right place for our bookshop.'

Bourton doesn't have particularly good views either lying as it does in the valley of the delightful River Windrush, but it does have the river. Sometimes called the 'Venice of the Cotswolds' Bourton is a gem of a place, cheerfully combining Cotswold stone with ducks. It is a magnet for coach parties and has, over the years, supplemented its basic attractions with a model village, a bird sanctuary with real penguins, a motor museum and more. The river Windrush — shallow, clear, and moderately wide — is enhanced by pretty bridges that skim over its glassy surface. It is generally claimed by Stow people that Bourton attracts a lower class of tourist, that it is brash and venal whereas Stow is aristocratic and disdainful of lucre. Maybe so, but tourist money is the same regardless of the class of the visitors and it quite clear which town is getting the bigger share. At the end of the summer season Bourton looks literally worn out, the grassy slopes beside the river patched with bald spots.

Like Stow, Bourton has its crop of dependent villages, including Cold Aston, Notgrove, Clapton-on-the-Hill, the Rissingtons, and the Slaughters. The latter being the most attractive and probably the most visited of the smaller villages in the area. They are quite inspiring and like Bourton itself are enhanced by the burbling streams that pass through them.

Though Stow, Bourton and Moreton are all within a few kilometres of each other, the distance to other Cotswold market towns, such as Northleach, Andoversford, Chipping

Bourton-on-the-Water

Norton and Chipping Campden, is much greater. Naturally all of these battle it out for their share of the tourist pie, the star, the town to which many are drawn, being Chipping Campden. Claiming to have the most beautiful high street in England this town does offer stiff competition. From its wonderfully large church to the clean cut and bulbous topiary on the southern approach, from its grand, and exquisitely maintained, thatched stone houses and characterful and gracefully arched market hall, it offers a feast to the eye and is topped by a plethora of intellectual activities from music to the arts. I have walked from Stow to Chipping Campden; it is not that far and provides a

Moreton-in-Marsh

superb Cotswold excursion. However, the places are sufficiently far enough away from each other to prevent any great interdependence, though they are undoubtedly major competitors for the tourist's pound.

Fans of Stow, particularly my wife, can often be heard proclaiming the convenience of its location. 'It is easy to get to Cheltenham, Cirencester, Oxford, Stratford, Evesham and so on. They are all a similar distance away', my wife tells me with a Hobnob smile. Of course this is a matter of perspective. I might put it differently by saying that Stow is nowhere near anywhere of significance. If it were a dormitory town of Oxford then it would be conveniently near the city. In fact it is inconveniently placed for any of the towns and cities around it. It is not (thank heavens) near a functioning motorway and its remoteness breeds a certain degree of independence and, at times, creates a mutual support centre with its two close neighbours, Bourton and Moreton.

Cheltenham, the festival and racing town, is Stow's true parent. There is a local bus service to ferry people to the big town shops and other attractions. For those looking for a good night out then Cheltenham has the usual selection of pubs and clubs plus theatres and cinemas and if you travel by bus you are assured an early night — the last one leaves Cheltenham for Stow at around six. Youngsters wishing to go clubbing together sometimes hire a taxi for the night, which sets them back something like £150. Oxford is a little more distant than Cheltenham and, residing in another county, has no direct public transport links with Stow.

Both of Stow's neighbouring towns have minor connections with the Civil War. In Moreton Charles I stayed in the White Hart Royal Hotel during 1644, and in Bourton the King and his son stayed in the manor house with his army camping on what are now the playing fields of the Cotswold School. The manor house was the home of Thomas Temple, the Rector of Bourton and also chaplain to the royal household.

In the property stakes Moreton comes top according to a *Weekend Telegraph* survey. It is in the upper ten of the small market towns in Britain. The *Weekend Telegraph* positively glows about the place saying:

> Moreton-in-Marsh is a Cotswold beauty with a glorious main street of golden stone houses with back lanes running off. Strategically placed between Stratford-upon-Avon, Evesham, Bath and Oxford, it once thrived as a coaching stop, but now attracts commuters who use the local station for the 90 minute journey into London.

Ha! So it's the strategic placing and that important railway station that did the business. In fact, Moreton is a pretty much a ribbon town with the Fosse Way slicing right through the middle of it. Houses are generally cheaper there than in Stow, which was placed in the top fifty of the survey along with Cheltenham.

CHAPTER 6

WHO'S IN CHARGE?

In King Charles I's mind things were probably quite simple. God had appointed him through his birthright to lead Britain, so what was the problem? Money, as ever, was the problem. Parliament was responsible for raising and collecting taxes — and collectively they did not see the leadership business quite as simply as their King — not at all. They wanted a slice of the power cake and were not at all convinced of any god-given rights the King might claim; in fact, many of them were pretty much opposed to the godly arrangements in the kingdom anyway, particularly the power of the bishops.

This was a time of great change in the governmental structure of England. Power was shifting. In earlier years both the Lords and Commons were predominantly consultative bodies, the former's dominance declining as the economic power of commoners grew. Traditionally the King appointed his own ministers and these were the men who had the King's ear. Charles' attempts to rule without parliament repeatedly ended in financially compelled recalls and the reconstituted parliaments demanding more and more from the King for his pot of gold — including a veto over the selection of ministers. This period was a clear forerunner of the time when ministers were appointed by parliament and the prime minister began to replace the monarch as the ultimate leader of the country. It was Charles' need for money and parliament's desire for power that ultimately led to the Civil War.

In the twenty-first century, money is still a major problem. Many resent the sums of money voted annually to the Queen and royal family, their resentment is kindled every year as the media pour over the civil list in an annual festival of surprise at the cost of royalty. Taxation is efficiently collected but many would claim that the vast sums received are neither efficiently nor sensibly spent. The reputation of parliament suffered a severe denting lately as the *Daily Telegraph* regularly and devastatingly leaked more and more appalling tales of MPs' expenses ranging from one politician's need to clean out his moat to another's bill for pornographic videos.

On the local front the battle for power and money centre, not surprisingly, on local issues, issues that directly affect people's lives and over which they have some influence. We may be much better informed nowadays, but the workings of Westminster are still remote. In Stow on the Wold the major battle is between the town and district council.

Stow has a mayor! It's simply a matter of size I believe, if the population were to fall then the title could be parish chairman, which is nowhere near as impressive. The current mayor is Robin Jones, born in London but having lived in the town for more than ten years. A sincere man, he told me with great humility that he does the job because, 'no one else would'. There are eleven councillors and they all do the job for love. They are public spirited, have an interest in local affairs and often have the luxury of time on their hands to devote to such things. Their major bugbear is the Cotswold District Council, who, according to Robin Jones, 'do not treat us properly' and for them, 'everything is about money'.

The district council is located at Cirencester. This is a much bigger place located some twenty miles away down the Fosse Way, Stow's major road. The towns have little or nothing in common except that they are both in the Cotswolds and are both in the district council's area. Stow people would automatically look to Cheltenham for a night out, a day's shopping or a day at the races — not to Cirencester.

Stow and a few of the nearby villages share two district councillors and one of them, David Penman, lives around the corner from me. He is a conservative, nearly all of the forty-four councillors are — this is the Cotswolds after all. He is chairman of the omnipotent Overview and Scrutiny Committee amongst other things and is almost overwhelmed at times by the work involved. He is supposed to devote four hours a week to the task but tells me that it consumes much, much more of his time. He thinks that Stow is a 'frustrating place' and I believe that he is not alone in that view.

Robin thinks that Stow is 'rurally deprived' but when I put this view to David he responded, 'not really, no more than anywhere else'. I tend to agree with the district councillor — after all this town does have a Tesco supermarket, how rurally deprived is that? However, as previously described, it would not have a Tesco if a vocal and influential group of locals had had their way. Perhaps this is what makes Stow 'frustrating'?

My ears pricked up at the term 'rurally deprived', it sounded rather official — the sort of thing that local government officials might say (like 'joined up thinking', 'stakeholder engagement' and 'going forward'). I did a little research and found the same term in the publications of the Commission for Rural Communities and in many other local government publications. I was impressed to see that there is actually a Peak District Rural Deprivation Forum! But nowhere could I find a definition of what the hell it is. I think I know what deprivation is and I supposed that the rural bit means deprivation in small places — rural is defined as anywhere with a population of less than 10,000 people apparently. So that's it — 'rural deprivation' is a different form of deprivation to that which you might encounter in say, Oxford, or some other large place. Then I read in one report that 'urban and rural categorisations are largely becoming irrelevant as people live their lives in different ways rendering conventional definitions obsolete.' So I concluded that I was wasting my time. But still I wanted to know what rural deprivation might mean, and after all, if I am rurally deprived I should like to know what I'm missing.

I asked the mayor for examples of rural deprivation in Stow. His immediate response was based on a recent emergency involving the town clerk. This poor man had a heart attack and had to wait for over half an hour before the ambulance arrived. The clerk did survive, but subsequently resigned his post. I asked for other examples of deprivation and Robin suggested that broadband access to the Internet was too slow and there was a lack of affordable housing. Discussing these points with the District Councillor was revealing. He too was concerned about the time taken for an ambulance to arrive but talked of a new scheme that tries to ensure that someone responds to an emergency call within minutes. However, this speedy scheme does rely on local volunteers who are trained to deal with emergencies until the big boys arrive in the ambulance. Apparently, at the time of writing, no one from Stow has volunteered for this service — hopefully they will. On the broadband issue David said that it is available in Stow and is not likely to be slower than anywhere else. The third deprivation — affordable housing — is a hot topic nearly everywhere, especially in places like Oxford where inflated house prices drive the less well off to find homes well beyond the city or simply drives them away. Undoubtedly Stow has similar problems and I will return to them later, but it's pretty clear that these problems are not unique to the town or indeed to the country. So maybe Stow is not deprived, merely rural.

Any attempt to discuss local democracy soon moves from the particular to the general and then leaps onward to the question of democracy in general. I am not going to take that leap, but I do want to touch on some general points about local democracy. Firstly, most people take no part in it. According to a recent survey in rural England less than half the rural population felt that they could influence local decisions at all, and three-quarters of people had never approached their local councillors. What is more, most people had little or no idea of what their local council did! Yet, viewed from the other side of the same coin, only a very small number of councillors thought that they had not been effective in their role. Bit of a mismatch here I think — but no surprises.

I sense a frustration in both town and district councillors which stems to a large degree from their inability to act on most issues. For ten years now I have lived part of my life in a small Spanish village — much smaller than Stow. One of the most noticeable buildings in my village is the town hall, which dominates the main square. It is a functional building with a council meeting room and a large office in which the mayor can be seen signing papers (when he is not roaring around the village on his scooter or busy doing whatever he does on his large tractor). The town clerk also has an office there and both he and the mayor can be observed in the thick of things. Recently the streets around my house have been torn up in order to install new drains and water mains. The mayor could be seen in the trenches and I spotted the town clerk (who also collects the rubbish) wielding a pickaxe as he sorted out a problem at the confluence of three streets. In this village plans to build new houses and renovate old ones are dealt with by the local council and taxes are raised locally. The point is that the mayor and the clerk and the councillors have real power. According to John Kennell, a Stow councillor for nine years, the town council of Stow is powerless over most issues. It does have responsibility for burials and children's playgrounds, but that's about all — it does not even have a town hall.

The hall, which most visitors would assume to be Stow's town hall, is called St Edward's Hall and its tall Victorian-gothic structure dominates the square. Far from being a council property, it was funded by dead accounts. Back in the nineteenth century, the local bank was found to have a significant sum of money in accounts that no longer had owners so, very imaginatively, the deposits were used to create the existing hall. It is run by trustees and maintained by the county council who, in return, pay only a peppercorn rent for the ground floor, which it operates as a library.

St Edward's Hall

In contrast to the town council the district council does have power: it controls important things like planning, housing, and leisure. Yes it has power, a big budget, a few hundred staff and lots of offices, but it's dilute. Things of concern to Stow are represented by just two councillors out of forty-four. Put it another way: forty-two councillors who are not from Stow have a say over issues which are of direct concern to the place as against two who are from the town. Of course this is not just an issue for Stow, it's a problem of representative democracy. But it is still frustrating for the representatives and a little demeaning too. Having gone to the bother of getting themselves elected their ability to do anything about Mrs Smith's blocked drain, or Mr Jones' noisy neighbour, or the plan to build a supermarket is often much less than that of a pressure group formed to tackle any of these subjects — even Mrs Smith's drains.

Of course the really big things, and the really big money, are managed by the county council. Gloucestershire County Council in the case of Stow. It looks after the police, schooling, highways, and so on. Funnily enough there doesn't seem to be a battle here. Either these issues are too remote to bother with or the councillor's doing a grand job. In any event the complaint level is low. The main battle seems to be between town and district and, in the background, between representatives and represented.

Let battle commence. Take parking — oh no, not parking, the one subject that a good friend who was a councillor in Oxford at one time said that you should avoid at all costs! Stow has lots of car parking. Why, on Christmas Day the place looks positively denuded with so few cars and no coaches in the square and the two peripheral car parks lying empty. However, in the high season there is often nowhere to park and for the local popping into town to visit the farmer's market, or Scotts of Stow, or the superior butchers in Digbeth Street, this is supremely frustrating — to the point of anger. So what's to be done?

Here, as John Kennell explained to me, is a good example of how the district and the town councils see things differently. As far as the district is concerned the solution to the problem is to charge for parking — at present the square is a free parking zone. Once again, according to John and in the words of Mandy Rice Davies, 'they would say that wouldn't they'. After all they have a financial problem: a huge hole in their pension fund. Any income that can be dropped into that hole is very welcome. Second of all they have a particular attitude to tourists: make 'em pay. Why not? Tourists come to the town, enjoy the sights, visit the church, and sit in the stocks. Why shouldn't they pay to park? The town has a different view, or at least the traders of the town do. They want to encourage the visitors. Visitors bring money to the town, they spend in the shops, they drink in the pubs, they eat in the restaurants, take tea in the teashops — and so on. Make them pay for parking and they are likely to go elsewhere. Then what about the people who work in the shops and pubs and so on — where are they going to park? Why should they have to pay? Start charging and they, together with local shoppers, begin to park in the residential streets around the square, and then the residents complain. And so somebody suggests a residents parking scheme, but it costs money to administrate the scheme so the residents have to pay to park in their own streets — then everyone is unhappy. But the hole in the district's pension scheme is just that little bit smaller.

There are two peripheral car parks in Stow: one next to Tesco, the other behind the vets. The district council decided to impose charges for these, despite protests from the town council. But the best-laid plans sometimes implode. In the tortuous process of granting planning permission for the supermarket, Tesco was required to provide a public car park in addition to the one it supplied for the shoppers. It did so and accepted the condition that the public car park should be free. So now the town has one free car park and one that charges — how odd. Is this the great British compromise in action? Meanwhile, plans are afoot to place parking meters in the square. And so the battles rumble on. And on. More of this later — I haven't even mentioned the toilets yet, or the visitor information centre.

CHAPTER 7

ESSENTIAL WORSHIP

To non-believers the world splits quite neatly into the religious and those who, like themselves, are not religious. What amazes the non-believer is the incredible variety of beliefs amongst the believers. In a popular hymn entitled 'The Church's One Foundation' the famous line 'By schisms rent asunder' appears in the third verse. Many of those schisms occurred at and around the time of the Civil War, about a century after Henry VIII had divorced himself from Catherine of Aragon and England from Rome. The Civil War was fought at a time not just of governmental decay — the Church of England was also under strain. Naturally there were fault lines along the old Catholic protestant divide, but these were reinforced by cracks within the established Church: the strictness of the Puritans, and the rejection of the prelacy by the Presbyterians. Added to this there were many splinter and new founded groups including the Congregationalists, Baptists, Quakers, and Ranters. The latter were a particularly off-the-wall lot who seemed to reject everything that characterised conventional religion yet embraced pantheism, nudity, and amoralism. Ranters were accused of fanaticism and sexual immorality, and put into prison until they recanted. Ranters aside, all other non-conformist groups agreed that the bible was the source of truth, meanwhile interpreting the 'word' within the bible somewhat differently.

There seems little doubt Astley was a true adherent of the Church of England but was his king? Charles I was clearly a religious man, but he had married Henrietta, an avowed Catholic, and his two eldest sons, Charles and James, both converted to Rome during their lives. Many on the dissident side thought that Charles was edging towards the Pope, an opinion that was reinforced by the behaviour of William Laud, his strict Archbishop of Canterbury.

Why the fountain of divergent religious beliefs at this time in the country's history? At least one historian accounts the blossoming of sects to the removal of censorship. Thinking about censorship reminded me of my night in Worcester, the only city that I passed through on my walk and the possessor of the finest religious building that Astley and I would have passed: the monumental cathedral with its astounding mix of architectures. I have already confessed that I stayed that night in a B&B. I must also confess that I went out to drown my cold in beer. The pub that I had chosen for this foray is the real ale capital of the city: The Dragon Inn. It has a quirky landlord who has

The tower of St Edward's church, Stow

his own rules and, like Charles I was, is quite inflexible about them. On a previous mad-cap venture I had visited Worcester, amongst many other places, as a shoe-shiner. On that occasion I had been refused permission to shine shoes in the Dragon so had walked out in a huff without sampling any of the beers. This time I had nothing else to do but drink beer so I swallowed my pride and entered this really excellent beer emporium, only to find that it was also a bastion of censorship. I sat at the far end of the bar and studied a blackboard containing a list of 'banned topics of conversation' including one which with gushing irony (I hope) was 'Whatever happened to an Englishman's right to freedom of speech?' The rest mostly scored a number of topical right-wing points though there was one that did not fit this mould and seemed particularly scathing. It banned all conversations to do with trains, specifically listing train-buff terms such as 'multiple unit', 'axle loads', and 'bogie'!

Stow has the usual places of worship catering for Baptists, Congregationalists, Catholics, and, of course, Church of England. For the latter, St Edward's church provides a fine symbol, its tower visible from all the approaches to the town signalling its presence to everyone far and wide. In the last local census about eighty percent of local people claimed to be Christian and they were supplemented by six percent Buddhists, four percent Jews, and three percent Muslims plus a number of 'don't knows'. However, the most exotic ingredient in the Stow religious mix must be the Brethren. Generally called the Plymouth Brethren, the Stow community are in fact Exclusive Brethren and there is a lot in that name. They live a very different life to the rest of the world and they want to keep it that way. Television, radio, Christmas, and eating with non-Brethren are barred as is voting and attending university. For many years Stow has been a preferred location for the Brethren with a thriving and growing number of them in the town.

In the book *Shut up Sarah* there are many heart-rending incidents in the life of a somewhat rebellious teenage girl growing up within a Brethren family. One of the most disturbing of these is a chance meeting with an old man whom Sarah encounters when taking an unusual route home from school. Through their conversation she is amazed to discover that the man is her grandfather and that there is a whole branch of her family that she had no idea existed. Incensed she races home to challenge her parents about this deceit, and her father admits that the grandfather had been 'withdrawn from' some years before she was born. Sarah's grandfather had disagreed with the edicts of the new lead family, the Taylors, and had been excluded from the exclusive. This can be a terrible punishment, the equivalent of being 'sent to Coventry' or worse. Once 'withdrawn from' no member of the Brethren can have anything to do with you: you have become worldly and therefore evil. It has the effect of splitting homes, family and friends, and is the main weapon in maintaining the Brethren's exclusivity — protecting the group against corruption from within. It sounds heartless and cold, but it is not a step taken lightly. It is preceded by 'shutting up', which provides an opportunity for renegades to remove whatever evil has been detected in them from themselves. During this period they are barred from meetings but are regularly visited by the 'priests' (those high up in the hierarchy) who cajole, accuse, explain, and guide them back to the 'true path'. They can repent and may be restored. If they do not then they are 'withdrawn from' and that's it — your Brethren days are over.

A friend who was brought up as a member of the Brethren, but subsequently left, told me of the constantly changing rules and edicts that were read out at meetings. Most of these now emanate from Australia where the chief family of the Exclusive Brethren resides. Sarah observes the same regimentation. At one point she is invited to Wales to spend the weekend with a friend who had married a member of the Brethren there. She asks permission from her parents who then consult the 'priests' and all is agreed. She enjoys the weekend enormously and, whilst there, meets a future boyfriend (also verboten). On her return she is shocked to learn that a new rule has been announced which bans anyone from going away on holiday. Naturally meetings of the Brethren, including the international meetings, were excepted from this new edict.

Later, when her brother marries a young woman from Devon, she and the family are prevented from attending the service by a new rule that makes it plain that the only true family is the local Brethren, they are the true 'brothers and sisters'. These rules would seem to make it impossible for boy to meet girl, but there are always the meetings, and they are controlled, so no hanky-panky before marriage please. And, of course, the local Brethren do mix freely. There are meetings throughout the week and, reading Sarah's account of one particular Sunday, the Sabbath seems packed wall-to-wall with them — beginning at six o'clock in the morning! She describes a lunch time get together where all of the Brethren sit around drinking whisky and all of the sisters prepare and serve the food. It's a busy day for the Brethren, but a convivial one if the shouts of delight and lustful singing that leak into my garden from the one next door (belonging to a Brethren family) are anything to go by.

Most people are shocked that the Brethren drink alcohol, I too was surprised when I first saw the recycling box overflowing with empties outside a Brethren family's house. But a whisky bottle is kept on the table to 'to demonstrate liberty' and I presume the use of wine is sanctioned by the scriptures. On the other hand, pets are banned — one might become too attached to a pet and lose sight of God. Christmas celebration is also discouraged; the Brethren remember the birth of Christ throughout the year and do not feel the need to celebrate one particular day. That's great for the adults, but not so good for the kids who hear from their worldly school friends of the wonderful time they had, the gifts, the parties, the visit of Santa — and they have nothing to say in return.

Shut up Sarah was written by Marion Field who wrote another book entitled *Don't Call Me Sister*, which contains her own experiences within the Brethren and her subsequent withdrawal from the sect. Although somewhat rebellious, she is far less so than Sarah and describes with poignant feeling her pain in finally withdrawing from a tight community that supported, loved, and guided her for the formative period of her life. In her autobiography she delves more into the near breakdown of the movement in the late 1960s. The strict moral climate of the Brethren seemed to suffer an attack of 'worldliness' as a series of illicit affairs were unearthed, one of them between a couple that Marion had known in Winchester where she had been a student teacher. She was shocked and assumed that this was the beginning of a purification process initiated by the Brethren's New York leader, Mr James Taylor. A plethora of edicts followed, perhaps the most important of these was the shocking new rule that the Brethren must not eat with non-Brethren. This was an example of the selective and often misleading use of the scriptures to achieve a more exclusive sect, one that isolated itself to a much greater extent than before. Taylor and his intimates used a quote from St Paul's letter to the Corinthian church to underwrite the new policy. Corinth at that time was a pretty immoral place, full of pagans and sinners. Paul ordered his disciples 'not even to eat' with anyone who was 'immoral or greedy or worships idols or is a slanderer or a drunkard or a thief'. The interpretation favoured by the Taylorites was that the Brethren should not eat with the worldly! The implication that all non-Brethren are a load of immoral, greedy, slanderous, thieving drunkards who indulge in pagan worship is a bit harsh on the rest of the people of Stow, or at least on some of us!

This was a harsh rule. Those who ate with the worldly must be withdrawn from. A brother from Marion's 'meeting' (the name given to a local cluster of Brethren) lived with his wife and her invalid sister. The sister was a god-fearing Baptist — not part of the Brethren. The brother was called to account at a meeting of the local Brethren for eating at the same table as his sister-in-law. He was bellowed at, given no opportunity to defend himself, and was 'withdrawn from'. Marion was shocked at this behaviour, behaviour she regarded as unchristian and this, together with the sight of the great leader Mr Taylor clearly drunk whilst addressing a Fellowship Meeting in London, led her to withdraw from the movement (Mr Taylor went on to meetings in Aberdeen where in 1970 he was discovered in bed, naked, with a married woman member and accused of corruption. He died later that year). Her parents also withdrew but her younger sister did not. From that point on there was no contact between the sisters for ten years until Marion's sister and family also withdrew from the movement.

Interestingly, there is a parallel between the purification process initiated by Mr Taylor within the Brethren and the aftermath of the Civil War. Cromwell established a system of 'Triers and Ejectors' to improve the standards of parish clergy, which gave rise to many demolishing claims. One clergyman was accused of being a 'common swearer and a common gamester and a frequenter of taverns' and another of being a 'companion of scandalous women', and yet another slated as 'an enemy to the Parliament'.

School must always be a particular problem for the Brethren. It is here that their children are exposed to evil and to the evils of advancing technology: TV, radio, computers, and the Internet. However, their youngsters must be educated so how do they square this circle? For many years they have been given special exceptions from religious instruction and assembly, of course, but also from the use of computers and exposure to video programmes. Increasingly they have created their own schools, particularly for the older children and nowadays to include the infants too. Brethren children from Stow are now transported to Gloucester where children are educated from primary through to advanced level. The teachers are not necessarily Brethren but are, of course, selected by the Brethren. Nowadays the use of technology is not so restricted — but is strictly controlled, for example they do have access to computers, but via a private intranet without access to the public Internet. Video programmes are played to the children, but only those vetted by the Brethren. I have heard that recordings of the TV series The Dragon's Den are played which may seems strange but is in fact very much in line with the Brethren's encouragement of entrepreneurial businesses within the movement; the Brethren are generally known as good businessmen and hard workers. The Brethren own the agricultural supply shop in Stow, and though not all of the staff is from the sect, they are clearly expected to adopt the Brethren's controlled approach to dealing with 'worldlies'. The shop is famous for the politeness and for the helpfulness of its staff.

Children are not allowed to go to university with all of its evil temptations, but the boys can go to specialised colleges. Girls are expected to find work in Brethren-run businesses whilst they wait for a proposal of marriage and then look forward to life of domestic bliss, always in the background, always producing children (I am told that in Stow the objective is to raise a family of five), always wearing a headscarf when outside the house, dressing decently and leading a god-fearing life as defined by the current Brethren rules.

For most Brethren women this is the life they seem to relish, and they do not seem downtrodden and miserable. But some will rebel; some will want greater freedom, a career, and worldly friends. This is not allowed, and they then have to choose between their family ties and their own liberal ideas. Once again the book *Shut up Sarah* focuses on this dilemma. Sarah is constantly torn between her immediate family, her Brethren friends, and the wider world where she finds forgotten or 'withdrawn from' family members and worldly friends who are not the evil rapacious figures that she has been constantly taught to fear. In her story she does try to make a break with the Brethren. This is a difficult thing to do since she is bound by strong ties with her parents and siblings and, when she does leave, is physically pursued by the 'priests'. She returns but her family is 'shut up' in order that her misdemeanours can be corrected, and so that her father and mother can be taught to deal with her beer drinking brother and 'kiss the boys' sister.

The existing Gospel Hall

It must already be clear that the Brethren keep to themselves — that has become their creed — so why should there be any battle between them and the other residents of Stow (a mixed bag of religious and non-religious sorts)? Well, there is always a reaction towards a group that decides it doesn't want much to do with the community as a whole. That reaction can range between suspicion and hatred, and can lead to exaggerated feelings and actions. It is reinforced when the exclusive group is clearly economically successful (many Brethren families live, by choice, in large detached houses with substantial gardens).

The Brethren, though by choice separate, are also very much in the public eye. The women almost always wear headscarves when out of the house and are usually followed by large families. The men eschew ties, are clean-shaven, and wear their hair short, and they also preach the word of God on Stow Square. All of them swarm to their Gospel Hall in the early hours of Sunday morning. They run local businesses and offer employment to many locals. They own land locally and often seek to develop it. On the other hand, they are noticeable by their absence from the pubs, restaurants, polling stations and schools (infants used to attend the local primary school but, as mentioned, are now bussed to Gloucester).

A very recent example highlights the battle between the two communities within Stow: the Brethren and the rest of us. In the year that I wrote this book the Brethren

The site of the proposed Gospel Hall

decided that they needed a larger Gospel Hall together with a large car park. The proposal generated heated feeling within the wider community and a new battle began. For many years the Brethren had a hall in Well Lane on the corner of Chapel Street. The building stood on the spot previously occupied by a Wesleyan Chapel — good strong non-conformist foundations. They also owned an extensive strip of land opposite and decided to develop the whole lot for housing (creating another battle — but let's stick to the hall). They then moved to the old infant school on the Oddington Road, sealed the windows so that non-Brethren could not watch them 'breaking bread', and regularly filled the tiny car park with those multi-person vehicles needed for their large families. Like Catholic families of old they breed much faster than the constrained and contracepted Anglicans and soon needed a bigger place for themselves and for the Brethren of Worcester whom they meet up with on occasional Sundays. So began their search for a new site.

The favoured new location was a large field of some four and half acres next to the Tesco's supermarket site. Pretty much a derelict area, it was occupied by two Dutch barns, one of which had partially collapsed and had taken on the appearance of a huge injured beast, its legs buckled and its body scraping the ground. Behind the barns lies a space that has long been a favourite dumping ground for some Stow residents. A red, wheel-less pickup truck takes pride of place there, rusting quietly away with the broken washing machines, refrigerators, children's toys and oft-replenished piles of rotting hedge clippings. This is a fertile area, constantly manured by the dogs that lead their masters and mistresses across the dump towards the woods and cornfields beyond.

'I have nothing against the Plymouth Brethren', said Amy Edwards in a soft, pleasing North American accent. 'But they are a small number so this proposal is a terrible waste. Why break the boundary? And if you do then surely the development must provide something for everyone.'

She stood pluckily at the front of the crowded meeting room in St Edward's Hall, shunning the proffered microphone that burst into a cacophonous screech of feedback if held at the wrong angle. Robin Jones, the mayor, sat at a long table facing more than 100 residents. The mood was angry but restrained. Next to him sat another council member, a lady who said nothing at all during the entire meeting. Next to her sat a grey-haired lady studiously noting the proceedings, and rarely looking up from her pad and pencil.

The meeting had started slowly, like a car in the depth of winter needing many turns of the engine before it fires — but once fired the get together had its own fuel. The mayor provided some background to the meeting, which was received in absorbed silence by the crowd, a silence broken only by a disapproving hiss when the mayor announced that the Brethren had decided, on solicitor's advice, not to attend the meeting (they had been warned that attendance might prejudice their case). It was patently obvious that the

Inside St Edwards Hall (Courtesy of the trustees)

gathered throng were there because they opposed the plans to construct a new Gospel Hall. The MP bustled in. He has a strange, sailor-like gait similar to a man constantly ducking blows as he walks. He was welcomed, then announced that he was there simply to listen. The mayor, like a man sitting beneath a fruit-laden tree, opened up the meeting for comments.

There weren't any! For some time an expectant hush filled the great hall lined with its mammoth portraits from the past. Nell Gwyn, the voluptuous nude on the north-eastern wall, seemed to crane forward searching for someone who might say something. The chairman writhed and emitted a strangled laugh. Still no one said a word.

'Well, this will be a short meeting', he said, peering out at the crowd in front of him, scanning the rows of packed seats and those standing at the back.

'I suppose I'll have to kick the thing off', said a mature man with a half-smile. He rose to his feet displaying a tall figure and a ramrod back. A younger man (who I learned later, was the chairman's son) rushed towards him with the microphone. He took it with obvious distaste, holding it well away from his mouth to avoid the whistles already demonstrated by the chairman. 'I live in Fosse Lane,' he announced, 'and I am very worried about traffic.'

He went on to give a variety of statistics, which summarised the number of extra cars that would be using the proposed Gospel Hall site, and to tell us that he had been a Metropolitan Police Officer. I was impressed by the latter but somehow missed its relevance, though it did add authority to the numbers that he had given. If he had told us that he had been a telephone engineer or a carpenter his point would have been severely diminished. Regardless of his contribution and his previous employment, he certainly did open the floodgates. It was pretty clear that no one else had wanted to dive into the awful silence left by the chairman. The ex-policeman from Fosse Lane had the courage and the will to enter and dispel that silence. And so the comments began.

'Stow is a small agricultural market town. Why don't they have the hall in Worcester, not here?'

'Why should groups like this have a massive parking space? Churches don't usually have car parks. These people add nothing to Stow.'

'They will go further and further. They'll be building all the way to Broadwell [the next village after the site of the hall].'

'Point is that they say this is for community use — that is a lie.'

And so it went on, sensible comments mixed with misunderstanding and thinly-disguised distrust of the Brethren, some delivered in a measured way, some passionately shouted without the use of the microphone. The mayor tried to keep things calm by commenting, 'that's your opinion' or 'you should write to the planning committee with your objection' or correcting a point of inaccuracy, but the general feeling of the crowd was totally against the application and mostly against the Brethren.

The key comment was the last one made. The land that the Brethren wanted to plonk their modern-look building on was currently designated as agricultural. That's what the two redundant barns were for — agriculture, and maybe the abandoned pick-up truck as well? The point was that Stow is bounded by agricultural land that cannot be built on unless the new building has a community use. Clearly the Brethren are a community, a very strong one, so that's OK. But are they the community of Stow? Of course not — they're exclusive aren't they. In the words of a councillor at a later meeting, 'It's not going to benefit something of the order of ninety per cent of the people of Stow.' So if it's not community use it shouldn't be allowed. This seemed simple enough — but planning matters rarely are.

'The site should be used for Stow people. Why not move the fire station there? It's difficult for the firemen to get out from where they are at present', suggested someone.

'All the fire men are from Maugersbury [a village at the other end of town from the site] so they couldn't get there in time. A fire station couldn't happen. But a doctor's surgery would be fantastic wouldn't it?' replied a member of our valiant part-time force.

And so we entered a new phase of the meeting — the re-planning process. Forgetting that we were there to discuss the plan for a Gospel Hall, this was much more fun. The idea of a new doctor's surgery really increased the heartbeat of the aging crowd. There were many speeches of support, and this was really a community project. It was left to one of the doctors present to bring the whole project back to earth: 'We've approached the owner of the site before. It's really not on for commercial reasons. We just can't afford it. We would like to do it but only as a joint venture.'

That seemed a good idea. Why not a Gospel Hall and a doctor's surgery? A compromise was detected, and everyone loves a compromise. The proposal was quickly shot down. 'The Brethren won't share. They're putting up eight foot fencing and floodlighting the car park.' 'Plymouth Brethren are not allowed to mix. They've asked for a letter saying that nothing else will be built on the site.'

So the meeting ended on a negative note — but plenty of people had spoken. A lot of stuff had been gotten off chests. This was not a planning meeting anyway — that came next week.

As I sat through that meeting in St Edward's Hall I began to consider my own feelings towards the Gospel Hall and the Brethren. I didn't really have an opinion, not a strong one. I thought the building was ugly — it's a standard design apparently, imposed from below (Australia where the leader lives). But that collapsing barn was also ugly. The traffic argument didn't really hold sway since the site was next to Tesco,which already attracted a vast number of cars. However, the community argument did ring true. I live next to two Brethren families. They are polite, respectful neighbours, but a community we are not. I have been into the houses of my other three neighbours many times. We have had them to drinks, to parties, and we help each other in the little ways that neighbours do. I will never be invited into the homes of the Brethren; they will never come to my house for a meal. I am aware that I am worldly and presumably evil in their eyes and I do not much like it. I am saddened that there is a barrier between us, and that this barrier prevents the natural formation of a little community where we live. And through that argument I made my decision. The land on which they wanted to plant their hall was agricultural land and their hall was not for the community, not at all. But my opinion counts for little; it was the planning committee of the district council that would make the decision.

The committee was chaired by a bespectacled lady wearing a scarf. The application was pitched by a case officer called Mike Napper who worked for the council yet seemed to brim with enthusiasm for the proposal. He used his laptop and a microphone to give a typically corporate presentation. He flashed up a representation of the building, called it 'contemporary' and stated that it made 'reference to rural buildings'. What the hell does that mean? I once knew a man who wore an odd tie to meetings. Hanging vertically it had an interesting, asymmetric pattern woven through its centre. Held horizontally the pattern clearly spelled 'bullshit'. If I ever needed that tie it was then.

The tieless (but not tireless) Brethren sat together in the packed public area of the small L-shaped room in the town of Moreton-in-Marsh. My Brethren neighbour was amongst them. We nodded briefly. Damn, we could have travelled here together — not.

An Oxford Professor, who happened to live in Stow, spoke for the opposition. He had six good points on which the proposal should be refused. Unfortunately he put them in the wrong order. He started by talking about bats and, I think, lost his audience. The key issues were the inappropriate building and the community thing — not bats. I felt like shouting, forget the bats, they can't see, they'll like the new building just as much as the collapsing barn (which Napper had disparaged as 'not fit for purpose').

The Brethren fielded an articulate young man who was, of course, not wearing a tie and looked like a rugby player (is that allowed?). He put on a good show hoping to demonstrate that the Brethren were part of the community of Stow: they employed sixty local people, they had been there for many years, and so on. He told us that most of the neighbours who looked onto the site supported their plan.

'It's that bloody collapsing barn again', I thought. 'They all want to get rid of it. I like it and so do the bats. I even like the fact that it's not "fit for purpose" — should everything be?'

Sarah Foster (same name as the Brethren girl in the book *Shut Up Sarah*) spoke as agent for the applicants, carefully refuting the professor's six points without getting too wrapped up in the bat question. This presentation was followed by a dizzying succession of councillors who made points and asked questions, including a long speech by one of our two — Merryl Phillips — who pointed out that 760 people had signed a petition against the hall. She read her stuff — always a mistake — and I couldn't hear much of what she read. Some points got through to me though:

'No benefit to the community.'

'Doesn't benefit social inclusion.'

'Such a large hall.'

'Will not enhance the area.'

'Would ignore government directions and our own planning laws.'

Good stuff Merryl. Her speech was followed by lots of questions to Napper from the other councillors. Then the chairman summarised by saying that the issue was complex and a site visit was needed. So, no decision, but my heart was warmed to the chairman, this was good democratic stuff. The case officer did not get his way.

'Brethren's hall bid is rejected by planners' shouted the headline in my local paper. I didn't get to the final meeting at Cirencester, but the news had preceded the newspaper article hopping along the bush telegraph that exists for such things in Stow: somebody who was at the meeting called a friend who relayed the news to another friend and so on. In the odd arrangement of planning meetings, where the local councillors can speak but not vote, at least one councillor spoke up for the Brethren saying, 'There is no doubt that the Brethren are a part of Stow's community and therefore any building for their use must be regarded as a community building.' But this was refuted by another councillor who stated, 'It's not a facility to be enjoyed by local people but a meeting place for worship for a minority.'

In the end it was the community thing that swayed the committee. They could not justify allowing a building exclusively for the use of one religious group on a green field site outside of the development area. It did not serve the whole community and that was that. Or was it? The bush telegraph soon ran hot with the news that the Brethren were going to appeal, then with the observation that appealing was not one of their virtues, and finally that the appeal had been withdrawn or never happened (the bush telegraph does suffer from extraneous noise at times).

The battle was won, the community of Stow had its way, and there will be no Gospel Hall next to Tesco. But the brothers still need a hall, a big one apparently — they were planning a 700-seater. And the battle scores the lines more deeply between the minority religious group — the Exclusive Brethren — and the majority of Stow residents. There will be other issues, some over planning applications, some over personal problems, and some over new conflicts that we cannot predict. The Brethren solve their own problems by becoming more exclusive, and the more exclusive they become the more they separate from the local community.

Their attempt to maintain an exclusive world within a 'normal' community can be contrasted with the Amish of America who separate themselves physically as far as they can. Both routes have their problems. A recent edict by the Brethren banning the sharing of drainage with the worldly seems particularly bizarre. I'm not sure at which point the sewage can be allowed to intermingle, presumably at the main, so semi-detached and terraced houses are out. This seems to predict a greater separation between us in the future. Let's hope tolerance will win out on both sides, otherwise battles can turn into wars.

CHAPTER 8

LOCALS VERSUS INCOMERS

The four years of Civil War saw great movements of men around England. In the early stages the key central counties of Gloucestershire, Wiltshire and Somerset were fairly evenly split in loyalty between the King and Parliament. The choice of Oxford as the Royalist capital in 1642 and the arrival of Sir Ralph Hopton's Royalist army surging up from Devon in 1643 altered that picture entirely. These breadbasket and route-rich counties became dominated by the Royalists, and the Parliamentarians feared an onward thrust towards London. If that had happened then the balance of power would certainly have altered in the country, but it did not — the Roundheads retaliated. Nevertheless the king's army continued its dominant position in Gloucestershire, though the county town of Gloucester — under the resourceful Parliamentarian governor Colonel Edmund Massey — resisted all attempts to broach its walls and later became a launching point for the retaking of garrisons in Gloucestershire by the Parliamentarians.

The war continued in a series of inconclusive fracas, open battles and sieges until 1645 when the arrival of the Parliamentarian New Model professional army under the leadership of General Fairfax swept all before it. Its relentless advance into the West culminated in the battle of Torrington in North Devon where the remains of Hopton's army were routed and dispersed early in 1646, the last major battle before the battle of Stow. Though many garrisons were still held by the Royalists, their days were numbered as Fairfax busied himself with the mopping up operation.

At any one time during the war the make-up of an army, particularly in terms of local men versus men from other counties, varied enormously — though it has been estimated that no more than twenty-five per cent of the adult males in the country actually fought. Even so, a young soldier standing on some strange piece of England far from his birthplace could suddenly be confronted by a relative fighting for the other side. A musketeer called Hilsdean had such a confrontation in tragic circumstances. Hilsdean was fighting for the Royalist side during the battle of Wardour Castle in 1644 and was mortally wounded by a shot from the Parliamentarians defending the castle. Before he died he leaned that the shot had been fired by his own brother!

Such conflicts were not confined to the rank and file. Sir Ralph Hopton, who met with such success in the early stages of the war, met his nemesis near Bath in 1643. In a confused battle Hopton's forces attempted to take Lansdown Hill with the

Parliamentarians firmly entrenched at its summit. The Royalist losses were tremendous and Hopton was badly injured when a powder wagon exploded after the battle. His opposite number in this battle, and others that were to follow, was Sir William Waller. These two men had been close friends before the dispute began and later Waller was to write to his old friend, 'hostility itself cannot violate my friendship to your person'.

The last ditch Royalist army under the command of Jacob Astley was, by all accounts, a raggedy bunch. Described as 'hungry and penniless men... half of them 'reformado' officers". Reformados represented the remains of regiments that had been destroyed or disbanded: they were desperate men with nothing whatsoever to gain from a Parliamentary victory, and everything to lose. The soldiers were the men who could be spared from the Royal garrisons in the counties of Shropshire, Worcestershire and Staffordshire. It is clear that their morale was very poor at this stage in the war (many of them had not been paid).

The army that the Parliamentarians quickly assembled to face Astley was made up of 1,700 men from Hereford and Gloucester under the governors of the two cities. These were later supplemented by 600 more from the garrison at Evesham in Worcestershire. Of the total force of 2,300 or so about 1,100 of the soldiers were Gloucestershire men. At a later stage approximately 1,000 horsemen arrived to join the main force from the Midlands. Thus the make up of the Parliamentary army was mostly local whereas Astley's men were from Shropshire and Wales with Worcestershire soldiers on both sides. All that said the conflict that the two sides were heading for was hardly a local one — and Stow was a fairly arbitrary location for the last battle. The division of troops was simply Royalist versus Parliamentarian, so this was certainly not a battle of locals versus incomers.

My father-in-law was mostly a happy-go-lucky gentleman. He would have 'little truck with moaners'. However, he did once say to me, in a tone which certainly veered on the complaining, that he could often walk from his home at The Park through the alleyway, or ture, into Stow Square, buy a newspaper and return home without seeing anyone that he knew; this from a man who had been born in the town and, except for the imposed interruption of the war, had spent all of his life there. And he wasn't complaining that there was no one about. Oh no, not at all! He was simply observing that all of the people that he did see were 'incomers'.

Exactly how many of the 2,000 odd people of Stow are now incomers is difficult to determine. Some years ago a survey of older people in Stow showed that about a third of those interviewed were from outside of Gloucestershire. This would almost certainly have increased in recent times. In fact, there is a village quite near to Stow that featured in a TV programme on the subject of incomers — it was shown to have no locals at all!

Robin Jones, the mayor of Stow at the time of writing, is an incomer, though his wife, Sue, had grandparents living in the county. He is a Londoner but doesn't feel there is a battle between locals and incomers. However, he did recall an incident from a few years ago. At a meeting in the town a local got to his feet and cried, 'All that you incomers want to do is change things.' Robin responded to the man by pointing out that if it weren't for incomers there would be no town council. I'm sure he had a point, a point that applies to many towns and villages. I asked one councillor how many of the eleven town council members were incomers. At first he thought nine, but then began to have doubts about the other two!

Typical Stow ture or alleyway

Why is it that incomers take over local institutions? Is it because they are genetically disposed to lead? Is it something in their diet? What makes them put themselves forward as councillors, school governors, committee members, village hall managers, organisers of the annual fair, and so forth? Of course, incomers are also outgoers. They must have left somewhere else to arrive in Stow in the first place. Perhaps it is the spirit of adventure that marks them out as leaders of their community.

In preparing to write this book I asked incomers whom I interviewed whether they were accepted in their new environment — most said that they were not. This may be a clue to their predilection to serve. They are creating a community in which they are accepted: they are the council, or the civic society or whatever. Locals are usually in a minority within such groups — or not present at all. Locals meet in small huddles in the street and complain bitterly, but in hushed voices, that the incomers have taken over and that they always want to change things.

Would Stow have a town council if the incomers had not come in? Of course it would. It did so before the incomers came and it would do if they all suddenly left. Needs must, they would cajole and press each other into positions of power and life would go on.

And, no doubt, at some future meeting some local would get up at some meeting and complain, 'The trouble with you lot is that you always want to change things.'

It seems that a dog is an incomer's best friend! Walking alone the incomer will undoubtedly be greeted with a 'good morning', 'evening' or whatever, but that's about all. Like the proverbial ships in the night passers-by simply pass by. Possession of a dog can make all the difference, locals will often show an open interest in a dog, stopping to pat it, examine it and even talk to it. Naturally this can lead to a conversation with the owner and 'hey presto' a link is made and words may flow. It's strange that a dumb animal should be the catalyst that opens the communication channel between two animals who are far from dumb, but this is often so.

Whilst walking through Upton Snodsbury on the route between Worcester and Bidford I met a man with a three-legged greyhound. Recalling one of those little factoids I had learned from the radio or newspaper, I said, having first inspected and patted the dog, 'I hear that a three-legged dog is the perfect solution to the age-old problem of chatting up women.'

'Doesn't work for me,' he replied glumly.

'Why's that?'

'He only likes men.'

The vicar exercising his dog on the cricket field

And it was true, he really seemed to like me — the dog I mean. Naturally I asked what had happened to the fourth leg.

'No idea', said my Upton Snodsbury local with a grin. 'I got him from the Greyhound Recovery Society. He was already legless.'

Two strangers each with dogs are even more likely to get together. Back to Stow, where the most sociable place of a morning is that wonderful cricket field with its Cotswold views. People meet there chatting in groups whilst their dogs run around together doing whatever dogs do. I suspect that they (the people) are mostly incomers, but I may be wrong — they do often wear those expensive green wellington boots that incomers seem to favour. I met the vicar there recently and asked him if he was an incomer.

'Yes, it goes with the job', he said with a resigned smile.

In my early days as a Stow resident I once met an Irishman, a man who has lived in the place so long that he definitely has achieved honorary local status. I was running my dog and he was walking his, so naturally we talked about our dogs. Towards the end of our conversation he looked at me intensely and then said, 'Are you a local man, or do

The White Hart, Stow

you came from Broadwell?' I was taken aback and later recounted the encounter with wry amusement. We had met somewhere between the town of Stow and the village of Broadwell, hence his question. But the two places are no more than a mile apart! How local is local?

At the end of 2008 new tenants moved into the White Hart, a hotel cum pub with a prime location on the square. The previous tenant had been there for perhaps five years, had started well and then let the place decline. The front bar had been a favourite with a set of jovial locals, many of whom were also users of the British Legion Club just through the passageway.

I have fond memories of the place, though not of the beer! Many years ago it had been the final boozer on a pub-crawl to celebrate the stag night of my brother-in-law, Henry. We had established ourselves around the front bar for some time, loquacious and comedic — we were 'well-oiled'. At some point someone called out, 'Where's Henry?'

There was a pause in the conversation for a while and a brief search of the bar was carried out. The 'stag' was missing, and had not been seen since the previous pub! An external search party was organised and a small group of men in very poor shape marched out into the snow (I remember snow, though my wife maintains that Henry was married in the summer). The search was brief. Henry was found alongside the passageway, asleep or unconscious, on the concrete apron. The bride-to-be's brother, Alfie, kindly removed his own jacket and used it to cover the 'stag' and we returned to the bar to continue the celebration of his forthcoming marriage.

The new tenants of the White Hart came from another pub at Fulbrook in Oxfordshire. That's not far away, but they were, of course, incomers. They gave the White Hart a facelift. I did not notice any fundamental changes but the place had a smarter feel to it. It was less jammed with chairs and tables, the bar-staff were polite and friendly in that 'have a nice day' style which is redolent of well-run hotels, and the toilets were exceptionally clean and provided nice individual towels. I found it rather pleasant, though the old White Hart did have more character. Then I was banned.

I first heard that trouble was brewing when my wife forced a local newspaper cutting into my hand. She was, I could tell, indignant. The new tenants had closed and locked the gates to the passageway. Apparently they did not want the hoi-polloi of Stow using their passageway; allegedly some of the hoi-polloi had used the hotel's toilets and peed on the floor! Stow, I was informed, was in uproar. That passageway had been open for centuries. It was a public right of way and a right that all Stow residents enjoyed.

'Do you ever use it?' I asked my wife timorously.

That, I was told, was not the point. This was a matter of principle, not of usage. I was surprised at the reaction the closure produced in some residents. Blood was spat and pronouncements that 'Stow would never forgive' were made. The use of spray cans was seriously considered, though my tongue-in-cheek proposal of building a battering ram was seen as evidence that I did not really feel strongly enough about the issue.

A petition and a protest were quickly organised. Nearly two hundred of us (including dogs and children) assembled on the green around the emblematic stocks on a cold yet sunny Sunday morning. Was this to be a re-enactment of the Battle of Stow? No, the Royalists had wanted passage to Oxford, this lot merely wanted passage to Well Lane, the British Legion and the doctors' surgery. Not that much in common then, though I

Resident's protest outside the White Hart

guessed that the confusion was similar. No one knew what to do. Two reporters scurried about taking photos and notes. Photogenic children were arranged for 'realistic' news shots, often borrowing signs from the better prepared. One of the signs read 'Used by Stow residents for 100s of years. Closed by incomers in 3 months.' Someone produced a letter written by a YMCA official — their hostel sits on the other side of the blocked passageway from the White Hart. This pointed out that the YMCA was guaranteed unimpeded access through the passageway for its staff and their guests through its deeds. It was not, however, definitive about the use as a public right of way.

At last a lady in her thirties with a decidedly Midland accent, called us to attention. 'We must stay on the Green,' she announced with passion. 'The police have advised us that we must not approach the White Hart, we must not enter it. We must stay here.'

There were some puzzled groans from the crowd. 'Of course we can approach the pub,' someone called, 'it's on a public highway.'

The organiser looked concerned. 'Please ladies, you must stay here', she implored. 'If you do approach the pub you will get us, the organisers, into trouble with the police. Later we will be bringing around hot tea and chocolate.'

I'm sure she meant to say 'ladies and gentlemen and kids and dogs', but she did just address the ladies. Her pleas were as successful as those of the dog owners trying to prevent their charges sniffing other dogs. Many of us marched off towards the offending gates, Cathy, a militant friend, said that we should walk silently through the pub itself. This demo was warming up!

Nothing much happened though. Posed photographs were taken of the crowd in front of the gates. The police hung back, ignoring one old lady's cat call of 'Where were you when the gypsies were here then?' News arrived that the landlady of the White Hart, Mandy Griffiths, had been interviewed and was heard to say, 'They can protest as much as they like. I am not opening the passageway.'

This appalling show of indifference, true or not, soon got around. There was some orchestrated chanting of the words, 'Keep our passageway open', which died away after a short while. Finally after about half an hour Cathy went off to buy tomatoes, my wife went to buy other groceries, and I went off to buy the Oxford Times. The great demonstration had disintegrated. I had expected at least a speech and a protest march around the square, but I suppose the point was made. Battle lines had been established.

Letters were written to the MP, to the brewery, and to anyone who might intervene. Someone claimed that they had to make a fifteen-minute detour in order to get to the square now that the gates were closed. Nigel Drury, a local man, applied to Gloucestershire County Council asking that the alley become a public right of way. The MP urged people to write to the council and send copies to him meanwhile praising the 'wonderful community feel' in Stow, which was enjoyed by residents and tourists alike. The landlady said that if the MP had nothing better to do than support 'them' then he shouldn't be an MP.

Her resolution to keep the gates closed was strengthened by the reaction of the people of Stow. She claims that she and her partner were 'spat and sworn at' and that they had received a death threat by text saying 'open those gates or die'! The protestors, smelling a rat, asked how any of the locals could know the landlady's mobile phone number. The police later confirmed to the press that they were not investigating a death threat. Blimey, things were heating up. Was this a battle or not?

My wife wrote to the brewery and received a reply. What picture enters your head when you read the word brewery? Forget that picture: the Donnington Brewery is the most beautiful in the world. Imagine a large lake, with black swans gracing its surface, set in a remote dell of the rolling Cotswold countryside. Imagine a majestic jumble of mellow Cotswold stone buildings, including one with a water mill attached to it, all dotted around one end of the lake. Picture a graceful house with well-tended gardens. That's the Donnington Brewery. Everything is perfect — except the beer. I would like to like it, and in fact I used to love it. Now I am a member of an elite group in Stow, people who love the Donnington pubs and the brewery, but do not relish the beer. Since the aging Claude Arkell took his own life a few years ago the brewery has been run by a nephew, James, a member of the Arkell's family of Swindon, owners of the much bigger brewing concern and the company that own the White Hart (and, of course, the alleyway). James Arkell replied in a handwritten letter to my wife stating that he had enjoyed her letter, 'so much nicer than many we have been receiving', and he hoped that a resolution would be found but feared that much damage had been done by 'threatening and hateful' letters.

White Hart Lane, partly opened

The threats and hatred, demonstrations and accusations, claims and counter claims, did lead to a resolution of a kind. The landlord and landlady seemed quite unmoved in their resolve to keep the alleyway closed and also surprisingly unconcerned about loss of local support for their business. They claimed that they had always wanted to make a garden in the alleyway for use by customers of the pub. They did so and fenced off a small section to be used as a footpath. The locals had won — or had they? The fence is high so the hoi-polloi cannot intimidate the customers and the gate has one of those difficult-to-use code locks on it and is only to be open during daylight hours, and only if the hoi-polloi behave — but still and all, the gate was open.

This solution seems to have been developed by James Arkell, the landlords declined to comment on the outcome to the press. The mayor was pleased and called for an end to hostilities. That call probably fell on deaf ears. The outrage that surged throughout the town when the gates were closed had its flames fanned by the reported and rumoured comments that followed from the landlords, Mandy and Paul Griffiths, and were difficult to quell. In fairness there were some supporters of this beleaguered pair. A letter from that ubiquitous author 'name and address supplied' in one of the local papers suggested that the protestors themselves 'open their gates and allow a woman with four children and all and sundry to traverse their garden six times a day'. Why the writer singled out 'a woman with four children' to demonstrate the horror of turning one's garden into a public footpath is quite beyond me. The letter also informs readers that the landlords 'have got to make a living to keep the roof over their heads. Their priority is to please their paying customers'. But who are the customers?

I am not a customer, I have been barred from entering the place by that supreme authority in my life — my wife — and many Stow people, incomers, and locals alike have also placed a boycott on the White Hart. Some will never go there again, even if full access to the alleyway is restored. One day I saw a man reading the menu through the window of the place; he was suddenly pushed along by his wife who cried 'We can't go in there, not after the things she's said.'

The White Hart is a hotel so part of its customer base is drawn from visitors to the town who know nothing of the battle of the alley. It is being marketed as a good class restaurant and should therefore attract diners from out of town who also know nothing, or perhaps care little, about the battle. However, to antagonise the local trade still seems strange — after all, visitors are seasonal and the bar of the White Hart did once have its own local following, which kept things ticking over during the winter months. In fact, during the reign of a previous landlord positive discrimination was practiced. Calling there with a small party of visitors one night I ordered a round and was appalled by the price charged — more than I would pay in the centre of Oxford. The barmaid overheard my complaint and asked me if I was local.

'Yes,' I replied warily, wondering where this was leading, 'I live in the Evesham Road.'

'Oh sorry,' she said, smilingly handing me a refund, 'I thought you were a tourist and charged you at the higher rate.'

The current landlords seemed to have reversed this policy to the point where they do not want local customers at any price.

Meanwhile, the battle to make the alley officially into a public right of way continues. The plucky applicant, Nigel Drury, has been faced with a dilemma. The brewery has pointed out to him that the current arrangement for partial opening of the gates is for a 'permissive period' only, and will be maintained only if he withdraws his footpath application. He has decided to pursue the application, pointing out that he has no mandate from Stow residents to negotiate. He also points out that a 'permissive period' is pretty much useless as a long-term solution because, '… at the end of the agreed period the whole problem would just start all over again'.

Like me, Nigel has been banned from the White Hart, but in his case not by my wife. He lives in the lane beyond the gates and, at the beginning of the battle, finding his way blocked, decided to walk through the public house. Confronted by Mandy Griffiths, the landlady, he was asked, 'How would you like a public footpath through your garden?'

'Don't be daft, my garden doesn't go anywhere,' he replied.

'You are banned from this pub', was the response.

Nigel has gathered together a solid body of support for his application, including the MP and seventy-three local people who attest in writing that they have used the lane without interruption for many years. His evidence includes statements by two previous landlords to the effect that they had allowed unimpeded access to the lane for a period spanning thirty-four years. Meanwhile, there are others who state that they have seen the doors locked in recent years and that some landlords regularly locked the gates to prevent its adoption as a public right of way. And so the battle goes on. It will take two or three years for the council to rule either way, hopefully a working compromise can be agreed before that.[2]

Has the battle for the alley affected house prices in Stow? Seemingly not. *The Telegraph* has published a list of Britain's richest fifty towns, which rates Stow thirty-third. The survey was conducted by Savills estate agency, which reckons that property prices have been boosted by city dwellers searching for a happier way of life — a reversal of the historical trend where the impoverished of the countryside moved to the rich cities also searching for a happier way of life. The newcomers are looking for three key ingredients apparently: good houses, good schools, and good shops. It doesn't mention access through alleyways alongside pubs — in fact, it doesn't mention pubs at all.

As an incomer of sorts myself I am going to give the last word on the subject of inward migration to Ross Clarke who wrote the following in an article last year in the *Times*:

> ... is it really desirable that the countryside be effectively reserved for those lucky enough to be born and bred there? I have been back living in the countryside for some years now and can see that villages need incomers just as much as cities do. So often it is energetic incomers who keep the sports clubs and village fairs going — not to mention provid[ing] business for local builders and organic farmers.

---

2. Mandy and Paul Griffiths have now left the White Hart and the new landlords have thrown open the gates and extended a warm welcome to the locals.

CHAPTER 9

JOBS FOR THE BOYS

Though life in the seventeenth century was impoverished for most of the population, it was a century of change. At the very end of Elizabeth's reign an act of parliament was passed that effectively appointed overseers of the poor for each parish who could impose a local tax to help the needy, particularly the old and the disabled. Able-bodied paupers were expected to work and the overseers were supposed to find work for them. Refusal to work was not tolerated. Shirkers could be whipped and placed in a house of correction. The children of the poor were set to work as apprentices in local businesses.

Although the Civil War created havoc in all areas of life it did create work of a sort as men could become soldiers — in fact, many were forced to do so. Unfortunately the work was both dangerous and poorly remunerated, and paying the troops was a constant problem for both sides. The Parliamentarians were most efficient in gathering taxes but the effect on taxpayers was much the same whether the region was controlled by them or the Royalists — somebody had to pay for the soldiers, their weapons, ammunition, transport, and so on. Even so payment to the soldiers was often months in default. The New Model Army was the most reliable paymaster, the ordinary soldiers were promised 8 pence per day — not bad in those far off days when a labourer received as little as 1.5 pence for a day's hard work.

At first the armies were made up of professional soldiers, raw recruits and the so-called trained bands. The latter were an ineffective hangover from the days of Queen Elizabeth: a little like the modern day Territorial Army but less well trained. Local men of influence raised forces composed of friends, neighbours and tenants. Others were commissioned by the King to raise forces of horsemen or infantry. As the war became more widespread and its duration extended (at first the general consensus was that it would all be over by Christmas), then conscription became necessary. Pressed men were forced to accept the king's shilling or Cromwell's 8 pence. If they refused they faced severe punishment and worse if they later deserted. The pressure to enlist became stronger as the war progressed, and violence and the plundering of property became the order of the day.

For the family of a conscripted man the future was bleak, they had lost their breadwinner and probably later they would lose their home. Some wives upped sticks and followed their men. They joined a rag-taggle bunch that accompanied the baggage train of regiments, a bunch that included tinkers, whores, thieves, and was sometimes leavened by a few preachers. The hangers-on had to make a living in any way that they could, possibly by selling their wares or services. No arrangements were made for their accommodation, and both sides were embarrassed by the thieving and plundering undertaken by these stragglers.

Naturally employment was scarce throughout the land, but particularly in the Severn Valley area below Stow. The Forest of Dean iron works were destroyed by military action and the clothing industry was severely disrupted. Youngsters suffered badly in that apprenticeships fell to a quarter of their pre-war level. Those who depended for their livelihood upon access to the larger towns or cities often found them under siege, Gloucester in particular was held by the Parliamentarians for most of the war — as previously described it was a Roundhead capital in a county predominantly held by the Cavaliers.

The effect of the Civil War was not a temporary glitch in the economic circumstances of England. It is said to have accelerated the end of subsistence agriculture and decreased the number of small landowners, consequently increasing the number of labourers who owned no land at all. The war also spurred the move towards a money-based economy.

Part of Scotts of Stow

Nowadays there are not enough jobs, or perhaps not enough jobs of the required nature, to persuade young people to stay in Stow — unless their aspirations lie in the area of shop assistant or the hospitality trade. Unlike Bourton and Moreton, the town has no industrial estate to attract entrepreneurial rural industry. There is no hospital, no factory and no sports centre. There are small building firms and, of course, a number of freelance builders, decorators and gardeners. The biggest identifiable enterprises are Stow Agricultural, Tesco and Scotts of Stow (a multi-building store selling kitchen and garden goods and gifts). If you are an ambitious youngster there isn't much to attract you back after a spell at university.

In the country as a whole rural employment patterns are not so different to the urban picture. A recent survey showed that there were generally less managers and senior officials in the rural communities — as one would expect. What one might not expect is that the proportion of people in skilled trades in the rural areas was significantly greater than those in the urban sector — but do remember that rural includes population centres of up to 10,000 people. Stow, with little more that 2,000, is not likely to contribute to such an imbalance. In the urban areas administrative, professional, and technical jobs are much more likely to be available.

In fact, looking at the 2001 census statistics shows up some major differences between the Stow area and the national average, though given the town's special situation they are not so surprising. The dominant category covers agricultural, hunting, and forestry where four times the percentage of people work in this area in Stow as compared with the country as a whole. Ignoring the extremely small categories like quarrying and domestic servants, this is followed (surprise, surprise) by hotels and restaurants at nearly three times the national percentage. The overall picture is not all doom and gloom since the census showed that Stow had a greater proportion of people in employment than the national figure. Unfortunately, in a survey published by the Commission for Rural Communities in February of this year unemployment in the rural Cotswolds was shown to have increased by 22.3 per cent during 2008, nearly twice that of the nearest urban area — Cheltenham at 12.5 per cent.

The comments of one youngster from another of the Commission's surveys might paint a more vivid picture of Stow and the smaller villages and towns of the Cotswolds than the statistics can ever provide:

> The available jobs are either miles and miles away, or they get snapped up by more experienced people who are moving down to the country from the city for a more quiet pace of life. As a recent graduate, with less experience, I don't stand a chance.

We are in the midst of a hard-hitting recession, which means that in most market towns the number of empty shops has increased over the past six months. Around sixty per cent of existing empty shops have remained vacant during that time. In Stow my wife and I did a quick survey of the retail situation, we identified four empty shops added to which four others are now operating as charity shops. The mix of outlets and the sheer amount of them in Stow is skewed by its attraction to tourists; cafés dominate and seem to be on the increase, having easily overtaken the major trade in antiques. The gift shops probably come next followed by a range of tourist-oriented shops selling jewellery, clothing, shoes and confectionary. Fortunately there is still a butcher shop, a cake shop, and a newspaper vendor.

But as I write another battle is on the horizon, one that will affect all small businesses in the country. A revaluation of business rates is due to be rolled out in 2010 and for many this could mean a doubling of what they currently pay. As Sue Adams, the owner of the Coffee House in Stow, said, 'If my income had increased by one hundred per cent in the last five years then it would be fine but things just don't add up here.' She concluded that for businesses that have to pay rent and rates 'This could be crippling and in the worst case scenario mean closure.'

According to John Kennell, town councillor, the battle to provide employment for the young is doomed by the local plan that restricts development to within the existing boundaries of the town — so rural industry has little choice but to locate in Bourton, Moreton or further afield and gradually young people drift away. Added to this the young are battling for affordable housing against the cash buying incomers who have sold their properties in the cities and the aged who have done the same and bring their pension pots with them. *The Times* ran an article on inequality in rural areas last year reporting that the presence of 94,000 second homes in the countryside has helped to drive house prices as high as 9.7 times household income. Hopefully the recession has flattened that figure a little, but the barrier is still there.

This battle came to a head at the end of 2009 when it was revealed than nearly 100 households were on the district council's list of those waiting for a home in Stow, attracting the headline 'Fears Stow will die due to homes crisis' from the *Cotswolds Observer*. Councillors agreed that the way forward was to carry out a housing survey though it is not quite clear how this will cure an endemic problem in Stow and communities like it.

'I think the survey really must focus on Stow people with Stow connections', commented town councillor Moyra McGie. Adding, 'Because a lot of the people who can't afford to live here are people who work here or want to work here and people who can supply a crucial trade.'

The Times article was based on yet another report from the Commission for Rural Communities and concluded by saying that the Commission 'is not wrong to point out that declining numbers of 18 to 30-year-olds are living in rural areas. But surely this is not just because of high house prices. There is also the prohibitive cost of running a car: pretty essential for rural life. A village is a pretty rotten place to live if you are 18. There are few jobs, little nightlife and, in the deepest rural settlements, no one to breed with except members of your own clan.'

I do not think that Stow quite fits that bill. Youngsters do frequent the nightclubs of Cheltenham and they are still breeding. The hotels recruit friendly young people from all over the world, and, if nothing else, we have the influx of new genes twice a year as the travellers roll into town for their fairs.

CHAPTER 10

JUST VISITING

It would be quite natural to assume that travel in the seventeenth century was a hardship to be endured rather than the pleasure it has now become (for most people). Yet this was a century of great adventure. Of course they did not have the benefits of cheap air flights to Spain and other exotic countries, but there were opportunities. It was in this century that England began to make its mark on America and the West Indies commencing with a permanent colony in Jamestown, Virginia, then Bermuda in 1609. Perhaps our most famous adventure was the departure of the Mayflower in 1620 transporting dissenting settlers to Massachusetts. Then came the Bahamas and Jamaica and, in 1664, the winning of New York and New Jersey from the Dutch. Not all of the action was in the west: in 1600 the East India Company was formed and during Charles I's reign the first trading post was established in China in 1637. Of course there were many people who barely left the village in which they were born — but for the more adventurous there were incredible opportunities.

Travel within England itself in the seventeenth century was not easy, but it was becoming so. This century saw the rise of the stagecoach and with it the essential coaching inns. The King's Arms on Stow Square was clearly one of these as was the White Hart, though the latter's frontage was replaced in Georgian times. Oxford was essentially the route centre of England outside of London and had many coaching inns, the King's Arms (named after James I, Charles' father) in that city served the Gloucester route, no doubt via Stow. And so it became more practical to visit different parts of the country — at least for those who could afford the fares.

During the Civil War, Stow had many visitors and, as will already be clear, many of them were unwelcome. The King himself visited with a small army on his way to Evesham in 1644, and again in the same year on his way to Witney. On each occasion he was followed by Sir William Waller of the opposition leading an army of between 5,000 and 10,000 horse and foot. In 1645, the King was back again accompanied by a small force of about a thousand men. I say small, but given that the population of Stow was only a few hundred in those days even this 'small army' would have swamped the local populace. On this last occasion the King stayed at the King's Arms, which is said to have been first licensed in 1548, and today sports the arms of Charles I.

The King's Arms as it was

The Civil War was a restless time with armies and smaller armed groups forever on the move. But, of course, the movement had to cease at times; the soldiers had to rest, to wait for the next battle, to train, to refurbish supplies, to recover. Where did they stay? There were a few inns dotted around the countryside but nowhere near enough to cope with this amount of traffic. The only sensible solution, if they were not to sleep rough, was billeting — sticking soldiers in people's homes. Of course the soldiers were expected to pay for their lodging — but they rarely had the money. This led to the common practice of free quartering which must surely have done a great deal to antagonise the ordinary people against both sides. Efforts were made to allow householders to set their costs against tax, but the taxes were also needed for the war effort so often this offsetting was overruled by the collectors.

Everyone feared the knock on the door that presaged the entry of an officer demanding beds and sustenance for his soldiers. In many cases it meant that the householders lost their own beds and had to provide food that they could barely spare to a surly, smelly bunch of soldiers whose cause they did not support. Imagine a bunch of uncouth soldiers suddenly taking over your home, probably trashing it before they left, and then, just as you were on the road to recovery, another bunch arrives!

John Turberville, a Somerset man, recorded this painful memory:

My house is, and hath been, full of soldiers for a fortnight; such uncivil drinkers and thirsty souls, that a barrel of beer trembles at the sight of them, and the whole house nothing but a rendezvous of tobacco and spitting.

A Mrs Wheatley of Glympton in Oxfordshire was glad to see a bunch of soldiers depart her house in the direction of Gloucestershire but sympathised with whoever they might stay with next stating, 'They were as very rogues as can be, swearing and cursing like their father the devil — a wicked company.'

On my own journey from Bridgnorth to Stow there could be no billeting, and I had planned to sleep rough for each of the four nights as, no doubt, Astley's followers did on many of the nights of their march. I had a tent strapped to my backpack, a small, two-man job that was easy to erect and had a built in groundsheet. Luxury! I'm sure that the soldiers' shelters were much more primitive, though, as mentioned, they did have the benefit of campfires. I have already described my first night in the cold tent besides the Severn. My second night was spent in a billet. I was sent to the place recommended by a kind lady at Worcester's visitor information centre — it was, of course, a B&B, and a very nice one it was too. The house was large and Victorian, it was set back slightly from the city's main thoroughfare, The Tything, which meant that the delightfully decorated little room that I was given was rather noisy (the window would not close properly). Nonetheless I felt myself in great, and guilty, luxury even though I had spent just one cold night in the tent.

My next stop was Bidford on Avon. Finding a secluded place to pitch a tent that is fairly near a town is always difficult and I had soon passed wearily through the place, crossing the river Avon, without success. There was nowhere for a weary traveller to bed down. It had been a mixed day; the walking had been fine in principle. I had passed through lovely villages and gracious countryside — but it had been hard, so hard. In Naunton Beuchamp I had removed my boots and socks and curled my hot and pained feet in the coolness of the damp grass of the village green. That luxury over, I examined my extremities and saw that I was bleeding! The blood resulted from the usual problem of nails digging into adjacent toes. I trimmed the nails but knew that I had a painful time ahead. One of my sandals had broken so until I managed to repair it I was stuck with the unrelenting boots. Leaving that spot I can remember looking longingly at the seat on its quintessentially English village green as if I were leaving something valuable behind. It was some time later that I did discover a great loss — my mobile was missing. Thinking back, I became sure that I had left it on that village seat, but by then I had walked too far to return for the thing. Even if I did so, I reasoned miserably, it would have been picked up by somebody. Later I managed to find a working telephone kiosk — a rare find in the countryside nowadays — it would not take coins or credit cards but I managed to place a reverse charge call to my wife, asking her to bar the operation of my mobile.

Back in Bidford I stared gloomily around. On my right was the town's recreation and sports fields, and on my left some strongly fenced agricultural fields bordering the river. I opted for the public spaces. The problem here for a wild camper was that there were still people about; walking, running, playing, shouting, smoking and kissing. It was all too open, added to which a stiff cool breeze had now arrived heralding another cold night. I shivered in anticipation then recalled that I had bought a blanket in Worcester so

Cheeky camping, Bidford

things should not be too bad. I walked along a side road that led to the Bidford Sports Pavillion, a sad cube of a place built of red brick and topped by weathered planking that was in need of a repaint. The pavilion stood on its own little hillock and was closed, all of the windows were shuttered and there was no one around. I walked behind the building and found the perfect spot. The hillock on which the pavilion stood extended for a few metres behind the thoughtfully labelled men's changing room, and it was smooth and grassy. A perfect little campsite, it was sheltered from the cold wind by the building, which was itself emitting stored warmth from its brickwork — it had been a sunny day. The spot was not secluded; it could just be seen from the recreation field and faced onto a public footpath. However, dusk was falling, the park was emptying, the site was tempting, and I had no other alternatives.

I pitched the tent then went in search of food and beer. I tried two pubs: the first was called the Frog, a Greene King establishment, rather corporate and unwelcoming; the second was named the Bull's Head. This was much more of a pub with a strange cellar beneath the floor of the bar area itself, its entry so dangerous that when opened barriers had to be erected to prevent the drinkers from falling into the depths. During my stay there I was visited regularly by a small dog, a white curly chap who looked at me sadly each time he visited, then walked away. Later I found that I had been sitting in his favourite seat. I toasted my cold with a hot toddy then, satiated and slightly tipsy I walked back from the town in the darkness, looking forward to the first test of my new blanket.

Wrapped in my own thoughts I bumbled along without looking ahead. However, as I neared the pavilion I heard some noise and looked up. To my horror there were loads of cars parked in front of the pavillion, the window shutters were open, lights were on, and the place was full of people laughing chattering and drinking! What was I to do? My privacy had been invaded, my trespass had been discovered. I skulked resentfully past the parked cars and edged my way around to the rear of the building. My tent was still there, untouched as far as I could tell. Fortunately there were no open windows on this side and the door to the men's changing room was firmly shut. What could I do? Quickly decamp and try to find another spot? In the darkness this was hardly likely or practical. I just had to brazen it out.

I crawled into the tent and prepared for night, covering my 'extreme' sleeping bag with the new blanket. Of course I couldn't sleep. I could hear shouts from within the pavilion and was tensely anticipating an authoritative voice to order me to pack up and go. Then I heard people leaving, the usual sounds of groups parting for the night, doors slamming, some laughter, engines starting, gravel crunching. This went on for some time, then silence. I thought that I had escaped detection; I could now try to get some sleep. It was then that I heard footsteps approaching the foot end of my tent. They ceased and the tent suddenly lit up. The owner of the footsteps had a torch; he or she was guiding the beam over the tent, examining my little home in great detail. I dared not breathe. Then everything returned to darkness. The footsteps retreated and, puzzled but pleased I tried to calm my beating heart and settle down to sleep. It was then that I heard footsteps again, this time approaching the head end of the tent from the other side of the building. They stopped, once again a torch was used to investigate, and the footsteps retreated. I heard a car door slam and a car drive off. Was my late night visitor the caretaker? Had he gone to fetch the police? I waited, straining my ears for the slightest sound. There was nothing and finally, cold as ever, I managed to get some sleep.

By eight or so of the following morning I had gone, leaving that little apron of grass behind the sports pavilion cleaner than it had been when I came. No one saw me come and no one saw me go — but someone saw me there. I shall always wonder who the person with the torch was, and why he did nothing about my invasion. I'd like to thank him.

There is a constant battle in a town like Stow between those who welcome visitors and those who do not. The welcome often comes from those who benefit when tourists arrive, the resentment from those whose lives are disrupted by the visiting hordes. Though there are plenty of excellent B&Bs dotted around the place and a fair smattering of small hotels, Stow's visitors are more likely to be day-trippers than long-term visitors. They come for the beauty of the place, for the church, or perhaps to visit the Roman wells or, very likely, to wander around the shops in the square and elsewhere. Many of them like to pop into the visitor information centre to ask for suggestions of where they might go, where they might eat, to pick up local brochures, or simply to ask where the toilets are. The problem as I write is there nearly wasn't a visitor information centre and there is a shortage of toilets. And here battles have raged.

Go-Stow, the new Visitor Information Centre

According to David Penman, the district councillor, the Stow visitor information centre, popular as it was, simply cost the council too much; it was the only one in the Cotswolds that was run and paid for by the council. Unfortunately it made a loss of something like £80,000 each year and that's a significant slice of council tax. Others argue that it was supplying an essential service to many centres in the Cotswolds and that local businesses benefited from the service, particularly B&Bs. The cost of running the thing was, as ever, mostly dominated by staff salaries, but I believe the issue was finally brought to a head by the termination of the lease on the building used by the centre — a shop really, one of a row to the east of the square.

Reaction was swift, after all the information centre was well used. One B&B owner wrote:

> Bookings originating from Stow VIC made up between a quarter and a third of my income in 2008, booking around 100 rooms in total. How would guests find me if the VIC closed?

David Penman told me that the town councillors were asked if they wanted to take over the service, they said 'NO' without discussion (the expenditure involved would have absorbed the entire income of council). An obvious solution was to use the library as a shared facility; it's central, quite big and all the usual overheads are already covered. But the town council would not countenance this because the library is not open every day. David had his own proposal, which was to use the redundant ladies toilet (with toilets removed of course) as an unmanned visitor centre with brochures, Internet access, B&B contact lists and so on. A grant was available for this and the new centre could be staffed by volunteers if desired. This proposal was also rejected by the town council, perhaps there is something repugnant about using an old toilet for this purpose. In Oxford a pub called the Mason's Arms turned its old toilet into a brewery. They call the beer Old Bog and there are those who do not fancy it much because of the connotations.

An interim solution was found. The centre continued to use the existing building and was staffed by volunteers until a new leaseholder was found for the shop. Meanwhile, a local couple had proposed the incorporation of the visitor centre into their bookshop. The shop had been closed for personal reasons and the lease had been for sale for some time, but the owners were happy to reopen with aid of a grant and then run the place as a combined information centre and bookshop. This sounded an excellent solution to yet another battle between the town of Stow and its district council.

Sue Hasler, the enthusiastic owner of the shop that she now calls Go-Stow, told me that after months of waiting, phoning and writing she gave up on the idea of grant aid. It also seems that the money available from the district council for transforming the toilets into an information centre was from a different pot and could not fund her start up costs. Other grant applications got lost in the bureaucratic heap and so she finally decided to go it alone. The district council did not wash their hands of the whole thing — it was willing to pay for signs directing visitors to the new location and to include the Go-Stow address in their visitor literature. So, at the beginning of December 2009 Stow gained a new shop and a new visitor information centre. The shop sells travel-related books, including this one, plus items made in and around Stow. Sue is happily doling out advice to visitors and directing them to the toilets on request.

Ah, the toilets. I know it's not a topic to everyone's taste and certainly not a major concern of Astley's, or of mine come to that — there were plenty of natural toilets between Bridgnorth and Stow. The battle of the toilets in Stow was not about Old Bog beer but about sexual differentiation and cost. There had been two sets of toilets, one for men and one for women — and they were free. They were mostly used by tourists (mostly) and needed renovation. True to form the district council wanted to introduce charging and, shock horror, UNISEX toilets, just three of them, run by a commercial company. The reaction was strong and sustained. Prim letters were written politely outlining why a lady would not want to use a toilet recently occupied by a gentleman. More practically others pointed to speed and efficiency with which gentlemen can do their business in shared urinals. They created horrifying pictures of laden coaches arriving in the town full of people with an urgent need and hardly a twenty pence piece between them. By the time the queue forming outside the three toilets had trickled down to nothing the coach would be ready to depart, and the only thing the tourist had spent in the town was a penny (well twenty actually).

Seeming to add insult to injury, the British Toilet Association placed Cotswold District Council fifth best local authority in the Loo of the Year Awards for 2008. I do not suppose that you knew that the BTA existed. Well it does, and it has a website where you can browse the 'Latest Toilet News' or look at its sponsors. One sponsor is Healthmatic, which happens to be the company employed by the district council to convert Stow's old toilets to the 'Five Star' unisex, pay on entry toilets that tourists now have to queue up to use.

But arguments about toilets are not big battles are they? They are sorties amongst the factions of Stow in a war that grinds along beneath the surface of this fine Cotswold market town. Now is the time to slip back in time to a much more serious battle: the last battle of the first Civil War.

THE LAST BATTLE

I reached the crest of the Cotswold escarpment, pained and exhausted, during the afternoon of 20 March, the day before the battle. The end of my walk was still some distance away but I was nearing the battlefield and fairly confident that I would reach it before darkness fell. I had taken the old Roman road of Ryknild Street from Bidford through to Weston sub-Edge, the name of the latter proclaiming its location at the foot of the Cotswolds. This is the obvious route in the Stow direction and was the road taken by Astley and his men, though the main ascent road, Fish Hill, winds its way up the escarpment from the precious village of Broadway, the so-called 'jewel of the Cotswolds'.

Colonel Thomas Morgan and his men keenly observed the progress of Sir Jacob Astley, Sir Charles Lucas and their army as they crossed that unerringly straight road passing over flat terrain. They would have been clearly visible until darkness fell. The Royalists arrived at the foot of the escarpment at about five on the night of 20 March 1646. This surely must have been the Parliamentarian's preferred location for battle: they had the advantage of the steep slope and their men were fresh whereas the Royalists had marched for many days from Bridgnorth, and on that very day from Bidford. But they did not attack. Accompanied by just 500 of his total force, Morgan was content to harry the enemy to slow Astley's progress. Encouraged by Birch's counsel, the Governor of Gloucester had chosen the conservative strategy of awaiting the arrival of Sir William Brereton from Lichfield with his 1,000 horsemen. The remainder of the Parliamentarian army were left to feed and refresh themselves at Campden, 'which they did abundantly'!

One of the best sources for information on the battle is a paper written by F. A. Hyett, which was read to the Bristol and Gloucestershire Archaeological Society in 1892. It is based on eyewitness accounts, including a letter written by Thomas Morgan, the leader of the Parliamentarians, to William Lenthall, the speaker of the House of Commons, the day after the battle and on newsbook reports of the day. Hyett's paper is reproduced in Harold Bagust's book on Stow. My account is also based on Ron Field's excellent little book describing the battle and the background to it.

According to NASA there was a new moon on the 17 March in 1646, so the night, regardless of cloud cover, would have been dark. And, if my experience has any bearing,

The battlefield monument on its snow covered hillside

it would also have been cold. Astley reached the top of the escarpment at about nine in the evening, his army marching silently past the enemy who still did not attack. The Parliamentarians ceased their harrying tactic and followed the Royalists towards Stow after an hour or two had passed. Brereton, the senior officer of the three leaders, finally caught them up with them at about one or two o'clock on the morning of the 21 March. The three components of the Parliamentarian army were now united and there followed a friendly dispute amongst the three leaders (Morgan, Birch and Brereton) over who should lead the united force of some 3,500 men — each offering to give way to the other. Urgency may have been added to this debate when rumours spread that the Royalist were to be joined by the king's cavalry some seven miles beyond Stow. Morgan was made leader of the troops and ordered them onward to attack Astley's men from the rear.

But there was no rear. Astley had drawn his tired force of 3,000 men to a halt on some land between Donnington and Stow, which Ron Field identifies as Horsington Plantation. The plantation is marked on large scale Ordinance Survey maps as a swathe of trees bordering the west and north extent of a field sloping steeply upwards from the south. Nowadays it is approached by a footpath from the Stow to Evesham road that continues on into the nearby village of Donnington. On entering the field the footpath rises quickly to a plateau on which a cairn-like structure of Cotswold stone supports the battle memorial. Astley's troops were drawn up in battle order on this plateau; the memorial provides a diagram of their deployment. Finding them there, Morgan deployed his own men at the base of the steep rise: the Gloucestershire men under Birch on the left, the rest of his original force in the centre and Brereton's horsemen on the right. They faced Lucas, Astley and Sir William Vaughan[3], the respective leaders of the Royalist sections. Though disadvantaged by the hill Morgan had no option but to engage, Royalist reinforcements were approaching from Oxford but at that moment he had the advantage of numbers.

As twilight emerged on 21 March 1646 the Parliamentarians would have seen little of the Royalist force most of which was beyond the ridge. Nevertheless they charged upwards crying 'God be our Guide', the lie of the land being entirely against them, freshness and numbers being for them. The Gloucestershire men on the Parliamentarian left flank were at once overpowered by the Royalists teeming down the hill crying 'Patrick and George' and the Parliamentarians retreated in disorder, regrouped, attached again and were once more repulsed by Lucas's soldiers. In the centre fierce fighting resulted in a stalemate — it seemed at this stage that Astley might win the battle. Then Brereton, supported by musketeers, thrust forward with his cavalry from the right reversing the situation. Vaughan's cavalry were routed and fled towards Oxford in the vain hope of bringing reinforcements. The Gloucestershire men then rejoined the battle and the remaining troops of Sir Jacob Astley began a disordered defensive retreat towards Stow, the Parliamentarians killing and wounding any that they could along the way, including 'Gentlemen and Officers of Quality'. Most of the killing took place within Stow Square itself and it is one the fables of the town that blood flowed so plentifully from the square on that day that the ducks in Digbeth Street were bathing in the stuff (hence its name).

Sir Charles Lucas was arrested together with the other Royalist officers but Lucas was 'immediately rescued by a Party of Flintlocks' and escaped into a nearby wood. Sir Jacob Astley finally succumbed and, tired and saddened, was led to the Market Cross. There, in deference to his age and rank, a drum was brought so that he could sit down. It was from that seated position that he made his second great quote: 'Gentlemen, you have done your work and may go play, unless you will fall out among yourselves.'

And those words turned out to be so true. Cromwell and the Parliamentarians did indeed fall out as time passed and their Commonwealth proved short-lived.

The battle itself was over quite quickly, it started at first light, and the rout of Astley's army was achieved 'half an hour before day' according to Morgan. He wrote a brief letter to Parliament crowing the victory some minutes after the surrender at around six in the morning.

More Parliamentarians arrived soon after the main battle; a Colonel Fleetwood heading 1,000 horsemen entered the fray and rounded up about eighty fugitives, including the hapless Lucas. It is another fable of Stow that these fugitives had secreted themselves in a small wood above Upper Swell, a village at the foot of the hill on which

---

3. Vaughan is only mentioned in some records

Bloody Jim, near Upper Swell

Stow stands. That woodland is still there and is generally called Bloody Jim after its grim associations. It is a lonely place redolent of memories of the atrocities that are said to have taken place there. The few Royalists (less than 300) who did make their escape headed off to Farringdon.

It is estimated that 200 Royalists died on that day, including Captain Hastings Keyt, a local man. Keyt was from Ebrington near Chipping Camden and his remains lie within St Edward's church at Stow, marked with an impressive black slate tombstone. There are Keyts living in Stow today, distant relatives of the long dead captain. The burial place of the others who died remains one of Stow's mysteries. Lacking a prison for so many men, the captured Royalists were locked in the church overnight and then marched to Gloucester the next day to be paroled or exchanged.

It is not known just how quickly the sad news reached King Charles at Oxford. However, on 29 April, just over a month after the battle, the King left the city disguised as a servant, and Oxford was surrendered to the Parliamentarians on 25 June, the keys being handed to General Fairfax. One of the conditions of the surrender was that Sir Jacob Astley should be released from his imprisonment at Warwick. The war was over — after the battle of Stow there was no hope for the Royalists.

SACRÆ MEMORIÆ
Inclytissimi Ducis HASTINGS
KEYT. filii IOHANNIS KEYT de
Eberington Agro Gloucestriensi
Armiger Wigorniæ Cohortium ex
Parte REGIS Præfecti in prælio
iuxta STOW 21 die Martij
1645 OCCISI

Captain Keyt's tombstone in Stow Church

The war was over but times were bad. Dr Jon Wroughton writing in the history section of the BBC's website paints the picture so well that I am going to quote his words:

The war was over, but the cost to ordinary people in human suffering was immeasurable. Bled dry from taxes, they had also endured the compulsory billeting of uncouth troops in their houses, the plundering of their animals, the theft of their food, the disruption of their markets, the vandalisation of their churches and the destruction of their property. The lingering effects of the war were visible wherever you turned. One-third of the people in Gloucester were homeless [...] Hundreds of maimed soldiers and destitute widows submitted petitions to the county quarter sessions in the hope of gaining some relief. Fields lay abandoned; bridges broken down; and road surfaces destroyed.

This describes a very different world to the one through which I walked, exactly 363 years later, on my route across the Cotswolds to the battlefield site. As usual I took footpaths, avoiding the fairly busy Broadway to Moreton road and its branch to Stow. Though tired I was still capable of admiring the splendid Cotswold scenery especially as I neared Longborough and looked to the west across vast sheep fields rolling away beneath me. I discovered a direct route through the village of Longborough to the

Last campsite next to Horsington Plantation

location of the battle — maybe the very route taken by the troops. I arrived at the site at about six in the evening and erected my little tent in the lee of some trees at the northern end of the field. A man passed by as I bent to my work. He was some distance away walking a dog; both man and dog ignored me, but I had been spotted. In the growing dusk I looked around the field, took another look at the commemoration memorial erected by Donnington Parish Council in 2003, then struggled gratefully out of my walking boots and into my sandals for the backtrack walk through Longborough for dinner at the Ganborough Coach and Horses. It was very good — the dinner that is.

Stow on the Wold is where the wind blows cold. The battlefield is on a lower level than Stow itself, but still suffers from the same problem. I looked south towards the town and worked out where my home was, it was probably a kilometre or so away. I thought of the warm bed that awaited me there and almost, almost weakened. But it seemed to me that I would betray the days of painful trudging and the cold nights in the tent if I made a dash for home on this important night. I knew that no one really cared about what I was doing — probably only my wife was aware that I was camping on this strange site, just her and the man with the dog. I slipped through the cold wet canvas flap and into the chilly tent.

I could not get warm and I could not sleep. I had every item of clothing on and was encased in my sleeping bag and beneath the blanket — but the cold wind found its little entry points through the thin canvass of the tent and my temperature dropped. I tossed and turned and turned and tossed but sleep eluded me entirely. Then my hand touched something hard. It was just above my left breast. At first I could not understand what it was. It seemed to be small, thin, rectangular, and about the size of a mobile phone — my mobile phone! I felt around the area and found a surprise pocket, a pocket in my jacket that I did not know existed, and in it I found my lost mobile! Unbelievable.

And unbelievably it sprang into life when I prodded the 'on' button. For over thirty-six hours I had not known the time, now I did — it was just before four in the morning. I felt rather foolish; I really had believed that the thing was lost forever. There was no service on the phone of course, as my wife had asked the supplier to cut me off. I sighed and tried to get some sleep. I think I did doze for a moment or two, then the tent lit up, not as it did at Bidford, no, this was like being inside a stark white-tiled bathroom illuminated by a strong fluorescent lamp. Even closing my eyes could not shut out the light. My body physically frozen by fear, my brain raced through possible explanations. Lightening? No, persistence too long. Fire? No, too constant. Dawn? No, too sudden, too bright. Searchlight? What, here in the middle of a remote field? Ghosts of the battle? No, too fanciful. Then the light was extinguished. I listened intently, but heard nothing. I should have got out of my sleeping bag, put on my boots and gone outside to investigate, but I did not.

Sleep was now quite impossible of course. I lay in the tent, cold and a little bit scared, becoming aware of the soft pre-light of dawn leaking through the tent's thin walls. Finally I abandoned the sleeping bag, pulled on my boots and left the tent. I looked around through the misty half light. Nothing. The only explanation for my bright light experience was that someone had been in the field with a very powerful torch — at four o'clock in the morning — and had illuminated my tent for some reason and then quietly left. But why? What was anyone doing there at that ungodly hour?

I wandered around the field in the grey light. It was still cold but at least the action of walking warmed me a little. I tried to imagine that scene of centuries ago, the field filled with the two factions separated by the steep grassy slope. I stood where Lucas had been, on the right of the Royalists' central formation. I walked along the ridge imagining the progress of the battle up until the point when Brereton swept uphill to victory and the disintegration of Vaughan's cavalry. I had often wondered how the routed army had retreated towards Stow, thinking that their way would be blocked by the Parliamentarians. Now all became clear. The ridge of the hill runs away to the north and east, the soldiers would have spilled south along the ridge in the direction of Stow, the church tower of which is just visible through the trees from this point. I struck out in this direction, endeavouring to follow an arrow-like course into Stow.

No doubt in pre-enclosure England a direct route could have been taken, but for me this proved impossible — my way was blocked by hedges and fences, some of which I scaled, throwing my backpack over in advance. Then, with my own home in sight and clearly along the line of progress, I was defeated by an electrified fence surrounding a horse field. I joined the main Evesham Road and walked into the town along it.

It was still early, just after seven. There were few people about, most were still asleep. I tried to imagine how the town would have seemed at the time of the battle. No one could have slept through the sound of musket fire, the thunder of the horses, the screaming of the enraged soldiers. For the people of Stow this was not their battle, not really their war. Distant at first, the sounds would have drifted in from Donnington as the sun rose above the mist. The noise of battle would have declined as the Royalists retreated towards the town. But as the soldiers drew nearer the sounds of individual conflicts would have become sharper and more distinct. And finally the residents of Stow would have been deafened by the cacophony of pitched battle in the square itself, the wails of the injured and dying, the excited cries of the victorious Parliamentarians.

Terrified but curious, the people of the town would have emerged from their homes as the fighting died down, perhaps they would have seen Astley sitting on the drum near the market square, the spilled blood on the square, the soldiers of the King being disarmed and marched off to their jail — the church. Did they realise the significance of this battle to end all battles during the Civil War? Probably not, their main concern would have been the feeding and housing of all those Parliamentarian soldiers strutting proudly around the streets of Stow.

There is little to frighten the residents of Stow nowadays, some 363 years after the battle — except perhaps the annual invasions prompted by the horse fairs or a repeat visit of A. A. Gill. Gill, by the way, is not a reliable witness. On his visit of some five years ago he wrote that there were hundreds, yes hundreds, of antique shops. Well there aren't, and have never been. At its peak the antique dealer invasion produced little more than forty antique shops; now there are less than ten — and falling. The current invasion is by folk dressed in neat pinnys wielding coffee and teapots — there are just so many food and drink outlets in the town. And so change continues and the battles go on.

There will be no last battle for Stow. Many of today's battles that I have described will continue unabated, others have resolved themselves during the period of writing or sometimes before, others have yet to begin. However, all is quiet on the western front: the only gunfire is from the shotguns blasting away at pigeons or pheasants and from the muskets of the Sealed Knot as they recreate, once again, the last battle of the first Civil War.

APPENDIX: THE BATTLE
OF THE BATTLEFIELDS

Throughout this book I have assumed that the battle of Stow took place on a hill currently two fields to the west of the village of Donnington. There is a footpath from the Evesham Road (A424) leading to it which takes a north-easterly direction alongside Weasel Barn then intersects the Heart of England Way. After the intersection the Heart of England Way turns north towards Longborough where for a short distance it shares its route with the Monarch's Way (the route taken by Charles II after the disastrous battle of Worcester). The battlefield path itself turns east at the junction with the Heart of England Way, through a hillside sheep field and across a stream into a steeply sloping field bounded by trees to the north and west and with a plantation of young trees at its centre. This is the field that local lore identifies as the battlefield. The footpath passes the memorial to the battle then goes on to Donnington itself. I am told that the memorial was erected by the parish council of Donnington in 2003 as a belated celebration of the passing of the millennium. I will call this option for the location of the battle the Donnington site.

In recent years an organisation called the Battlefield Trust published an alternative location on its website. No particular reason is given for selecting this alternative, though one of the maps on the website does indicate a 'site of artefacts find', but the nature of the find is not known. The 'find' is to the east of the site, in the direction of the field described above. The alternative battlefield is said to straddle the A424 main road somewhat to the north of Greenfield farm. It is nearer to Stow than the other site. I will call this option the Greenfield site.

Attempts by myself and the Civic Society of Stow to obtain some justification for this location from the Battlefield Trust met with no response for some time, but contact has now been made and a joint investigation aimed at a final determination of the battlefield may be in the offing. In the meantime I made contact with the Battlefield Biker, a man who roams old battlefields on a large motorbike whilst creating his own travelogue on the web. He favours the battlefield identified by the Trust, the Greenfield site. He contends that this is more likely to be correct because 'The speed with which the Stow battle unfolded lends itself to being closer to Stow than Donnington, in my humble opinion.' And he has a good point.

There is some doubt about the exact start time of the battle. Morgan claimed that the rout occurred 'half an hour before day' and the Parliamentarian newsbook

Moderate Intelligencer stated that the battle commenced an hour before day. The three commanders signed their brief letter to the speaker of the house stating that the battle had been won soon after six in the morning. The Military Memoir of Captain Birch states the time of engagement as about three in the morning. In 2009, when I 'slept' on the battlefield sunrise occurred at just after six o'clock and I have ascertained that astronomical twilight (first light) occurred at 4.15 a.m. All of this suggests that the whole thing was over, from first engagement to surrender, in something between an hour and three hours, and this does indeed suggest that the battle was very close to Stow. The distance from the Stow Square to the two contending sites is approximately 1.5 km and 2.5 km respectively. After the rout Astley's men were either running or riding for their lives, tired as they were. At 10 km per hour it would have taken them nine or fifteen minutes respectively to reach the square from the Greenfield or Donnington site. Six minutes difference is neither here nor there. It's not really proof either way.

Contemporary accounts are not helpful in resolving the dilemma and it is important to remember that most of the people who fought the battle had little knowledge of the countryside that they were in. Morgan simply recorded that the battle took place on some 'unenclosed land between Donnington and Stow.' Birch's biography mentions the troops being 'drawn up in a field near Stow'. *Moderate Intelligencer* stated that the battle took place in a 'plain near Stow' (there are no plains near Stow).

In modern times, Ron Field, writing in 1992, has the battlefield firmly placed 'on high ground at a spot now covered by Horsington Plantation, about 1¾ miles north of Stow on the Wold, and about half a mile west of the village of Donnington'. But Mr Field does not reveal his sources. He retired as the head of history at the Cotswold School, Bourton-on-the-Water, some five years ago and attempts to trace him have so far failed.

A book published to celebrate the quincentenary of Stow in 1976 places the battlefield 'on the Donnington side of Stow, very close to the site now occupied by Well House Antiques', the antique shop was located in the village of Donnington. The English Heritage Register of Historic Battlefields which is available on their website shows a bounded map placing the battlefield within a large area which contains the Donnington site but not the Greenfield site. It is to the north of the minor road to Donnington from the A424 and bounded by the A424 to the west; it is south of Banks Fee (part of Longborough) and bounded by Donnington to the West. Local hearsay places the battle on the Donnington site, as did the owner of Horsington Plantation (unfortunately he died just a week before I attempted to contact him). The majority of local people when asked their opinion shrug and say 'who cares?' Astley cared, his choice, if he had one, may well have made all the difference to the outcome of the battle.

What was going on in the old soldier's mind as he silently passed Morgan's men near Campden and made his way towards Stow? He was undoubtedly puzzled that the Parliamentarians did not attack, after all they held the high ground and had shown every intention of doing battle in the Vale of Evesham. Perhaps he conjectured that they were waiting for reinforcements, but once again this conflicted with the belligerent behaviour that had so delayed his crossing of the river Avon. Besides, his every advance towards Oxford disadvantaged the Parliamentarians since it brought Astley nearer to his own reinforcements en-route from Oxford. One modern accounts states that 'anxious to avoid attack while he was on the move, he made the decision to turn and fight'. The last thing that Astley wanted to do was fight, he wanted to get to Oxford with his little army intact. However, it is possible that, given the weary state of his forces and the possibility that the enemy was not far behind, he was forced to conclude that engagement was inevitable. But would this wily old soldier have placed his tired troops directly in the path of Morgan's men? I am no military expert but this stratagem seems neither wise nor sensible. On the contrary, the option of secreting his troops along the pathway would be more advantageous. In that way his army could surprise, surround and overwhelm the Parliamentarians. Alternatively he could choose to rest his tired soldiers somewhere off the beaten track in the hope that the Parliamentarians would not come. He would then have chosen high ground where, if the enemy did arrive, his men would possess the beneficial position. The Donnington site suits this strategy well. The Greenfield site is on a much gentler slope and on the direct approach to Stow.

Frustrated by my attempts to solve what is, on the face of it, a simple dilemma, I dug into original sources. I found nothing to aid a precise identification of the site but did find divergent views of the course of the battle. However, examining Colonel Morgan's letter to Lenthall (the Speaker of the House of Commons), which was written from Chipping Campden at six in the evening on the day after the battle, provided me with a new perspective on the commencement of the fight. He wrote, 'I commanded 400 horfe and 20 Flintlocks to charge his rear guard, to put him [Astley] to stand before he should paff through Stowe upon the Woulde.' This certainly implies that Astley was still on the move when the Parliamentarians caught up with him. After a few words about the presence of the King's men beyond Stow the letter continues, 'where he made his choyce of ground, and had the wind with him, yet trusting in God, I drew up and charged him, whome half an hour before day on Saturday morning I put to total route.' I believe that this version of events favours the Greenfield site, though it does conflict with the description given in Birch's biography.

Perhaps we will never know the exact location of the start of the battle; in any event it swiftly progressed into a running battle on the approaches to Stow. No doubt the Royalists were forced to make stands as their hurried retreat took place so the discovery of 'artefacts' anywhere along the approaches to Stow is not defining. Even the route taken from the Camden direction cannot be precisely defined. The most used route out of Stow towards Campden would undoubtedly have passed through the villages of Donnington and Longborough rather than the Evesham Road (A424) as we know it today. We know that the existing footpath from the Fosse Way to Donnington was the main road between Stow and the village up until the end of the nineteenth century: the road is still present at the Homeleigh Farm end. Nowadays there is no road connecting Donnington directly to Longborough, just footpaths. But there was one. In an early nineteenth-century map the road is clearly present and labelled Bridle Road. It is also quite probable that the route taken by the Heart of England Way from near to the Donnington site to Longborough was a significant thoroughfare. It would have led the soldiers much nearer to the Donnington site. All of this would certainly have presented a very different topography to the one we see today and would inevitably lead to different interpretations. Roads in the seventeenth century were not well-defined; the definitive routings had to await the establishment of the toll roads which blossomed predominantly in the next century — the Turnpike Trust of 1770 defining 'the rather vague line of the road' from Burford Finger Post to Evesham'. Many of the early maps did not delineate roads, but Morden's map of 1704 does. It does not include the Campden to Burford road but this route is in fact included as a 'new' road on the updated 1708 version. However, Ogilby's map of 1675, though not at all detailed, does show the route roughly following the line of the present A424.

What does this battle of the battlefields all add up to? It means that we are not certain precisely where the battle began and, yes, there is a possibility that I spent a very cold and scary night in the wrong field! Ron Field's field. Take a look at my website (www. satin.co.uk) for news of any advances in locating the site.

BIBLIOGRAPHY

Historical and Contemporary Stow

'But is there any local honey still for tea?', J. Wheatley, *The Times*, 2 August 2005
Annual Population Survey — workplace analysis. Office for National Statistics, 2006
Article on Stow as a Disney World village, S. Davis, *Daily Telegraph*, 29 May 1999
Cotswold Observer, 18 November 2009
North Cotswold Surveys: Parish Profiles, Gloucestershire County Council, 1984
Stow on the Wold: an Illustrated History, H. Bagust, Aztec Publishing, 1979
Stow on the Wold: Glimpses of the Past, Stow on the Wold and District Civic Society, 2000
'The History behind Stow Fair', B. Russell, Letter dated 16 July 2006
'Three Cheers for Second-home Owners', R. Clark, *The Times*, 16 July 2008

The Civil War Generally

A History of Police in England, Captain W. L. Melville Lee, Meuthen & Co.
An Unhappy Civil War: the Experiences of Ordinary People in Gloucestershire, Somerset and Wiltshire, 1642-46, J. Wroughton, The Lansdown Press 1999
Civil War, Interregnum and Restoration in Gloucestershire, 1640-1672, A. R. Warmington, The Boydell Press 1997
Everyday Life in the Seventeenth Century, T. Lambert, http://www.localhistories.org/stuart.html, 2009
The Civil War in the West, J. Wroughton, http://www.bbc.co.uk/history/british, 2009
The English Civil War, D. Clark, Pocket Essentials, 2008
The Revolution and its Impact, C. Hill et al, The Open University, 1981
The Cotswolds: A Cultural History, J. Bingham, Signal Books, 2009
Stow on the Wold, 1646: Campaign, Commanders and Battle, R. Field, Design Folio 1992
Stow on the Wold Quincentenary: 1476-1976, Aztec Printers, 1976
Highways and Byways in Oxford and the Cotswolds, H. A. Evans, Macmillan 1905

'The Last Battle of the First Civil War', F. A. Hyett, Transactions of the Bristol and Gloucestershire Archaeological Society Vol 16, 1891-92

Roundhead to Royalist: A Biography of Colonel John Birch 1615-1691, E. Heath-Agnew. Express Logic, 1977

Military Memoir of Colonel John Birch, Roe (secretary to John Birch), Camden Society, 1873

The burning-bush not consumed: or, The fourth and last part of the Parliamentarie-chronicle, J. Vicars, London, 1646

General Background

Severn Way: The Longest Riverside Walk in Britain, T. Marsh and J. Leech, 1999

'Purchasing Power of British Pounds from 1264 to Present', www.measuringworth.com

The 2001 Census of the UK, Office for National Statistics website — www.statistics.gov.uk

'Rural Economies Recession Intelligence', Briefing note from the Commission for Rural Communities, February 2009

Also available from
Amberley Publishing

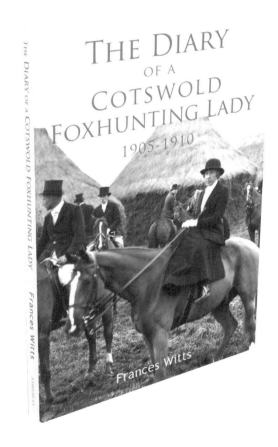

The Diary of a Cotswold
Foxhunting Lady

Frances Witts

ISBN 978-1-84868-020-3
£12.99

Available from all good bookshops or order direct
from our website www.amberleybooks.com

Coming soon from Amberley Publishing

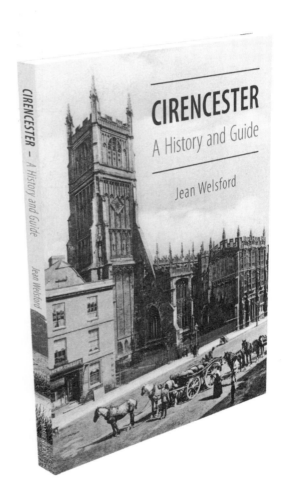

Cirencester — A History and Guide

Jean Welsford

ISBN 978-1-84868-789-9
Publication date: April 2010